Missouri Lesson Plans

MW01064680

McDougal Littell

THE LANGUAGE OF
LITERATURE

AMERICAN LITERATURE

McDougal Littell
A DIVISION OF HOUGHTON MIFFLIN COMPANY

Contents

Lesson Plans for Unit 1 Part 1 1
Lesson Plans for Unit 1 Part 2 11
Lesson Plans for Unit 2 Part 1 23
Lesson Plans for Unit 2 Part 2 39
Lesson Plans for Unit 3 Part 1 55
Lesson Plans for Unit 3 Part 2 75
Lesson Plans for Unit 4 Part 1 89
Lesson Plans for Unit 4 Part 2 105
Lesson Plans for Unit 5 Part 1 121
Lesson Plans for Unit 5 Part 2 133
Lesson Plans for Unit 6 Part 1 149
Lesson Plans for Unit 6 Part 2 167
Lesson Plans for Unit 7 Part 1 181
Lesson Plans for Unit 7 Part 2 195
Blank Selection Lesson Plan 215
Blank Writing Workshop Lesson Plan 217
Missouri Content Standards, Grades 9–12 219

The World on the Turtle's Back

Core Objectives
- Understand and appreciate a creation myth
- Identify causes and effects

MISSOURI PLANNER
Grade-Level Expectations
R1.C, R1.D, R1.F, R1.G, R1.H, R1.I, R2.A, R2.C, W1.A, W3.C, IL1.A, IL1.B, IL1.C

Integrating Skills

Grammar
- Diagnostic: Parts of Speech
- Parts of Speech

Vocabulary
- Context Clues

Preparing to Read
____ Connect to Your Life
____ Build Background
____ Vocabulary Preview: Context Clues   ❑ Unit One Resource Book: Words to Know SkillBuilder, p. 11
____ Focus Your Reading
Literary Analysis: Creation Myths   ❑ Unit One Resource Book: Literary Analysis SkillBuilder, p. 10
Active Reading: Causes and Effects   ❑ Unit One Resource Book: Active Reading SkillBuilder, p. 9

Teaching the Literature
❑ PE pp. 24–32
____ Reading the Selection   ❑ Unit One Resource Book: Summary, p. 8

Thinking Through the Literature
____ Connect to the Literature
____ Think Critically   ❑ Reading and Critical Thinking Transparencies, T1, T49, T51
____ Extend Interpretations
____ Literary Analysis: Creation Myths   ❑ Literary Analysis Transparencies, T24

Choices and Challenges

Writing Options
____ Essay on Harmony
____ Opinion Essay
____ Alternate Ending

Activities and Explorations
____ Oral Storytelling
____ Narrative Pictographs
____ Food Chain Diagram

Inquiry and Research
____ Creation Stories Compared

Vocabulary in Action
____ Assessment Practice

Art Connection
____ Every Picture Tells a Story

The World on the Turtle's Back

Teaching Options (from Teacher's Edition)

Mini Lessons

Preteaching Vocabulary
____ Context Clues

Grammar
____ Diagnostic: Parts of Speech   ❏ Grammar Transparencies and Copymasters, C61
____ Parts of Speech

Viewing and Representing
Art Appreciation
____ *Creation Legend* by Tom Two-Arrows

Assessment

____ Selection Quiz   ❏ Unit One Resource Book: Selection Quiz, p. 12
____ Selection Test   ❏ Formal Assessment: Selection Test, pp. 7–8
____ Test Generator

Homework Assignments

_____

_____

_____

_____

_____

Other Teaching Materials

_____

_____

_____

_____

_____

Song of the Sky Loom / Hunting Song

Core Objectives
- Understand and appreciate sacred songs
- Appreciate author's use of repetition
- Apply strategies for reading Native American songs

> **MISSOURI PLANNER**
> Grade-Level Expectations
> R1.C, R1.D, R1.F, R1.G, R1.H, R1.I, R2.A, R2.C, W1.A, W3.C, IL1.A, IL1.B, IL1.C

Integrating Skills

Grammar
- Plurals from Possessives

Vocabulary
- Using Context Clues

Preparing to Read
____ Connect to Your Life
____ Build Background
____ Focus Your Reading
     Literary Analysis: Repetition   ❑ Unit One Resource Book: Literary Analysis SkillBuilder, p. 14
     Active Reading: Strategies for Reading Native   ❑ Unit One Resource Book: Active Reading SkillBuilder, p. 13
       American Songs

Teaching the Literature
____ Reading the Selection   ❑ PE pp. 33–38

Thinking Through the Literature
____ Connect to the Literature
____ Think Critically   ❑ Reading and Critical Thinking Transparencies, T15, T32
____ Extend Interpretations
____ Literary Analysis: Repetition   ❑ Literary Analysis Transparencies, T24

Choices and Challenges

Writing Options
____ Definition Essay
____ Siren Song
____ Reflective Essay

Activities and Explorations
____ Oral Reading
____ Visual Storytelling

Inquiry and Research
____ Mapping the Music
____ Thrill of the Hunt
____ Hear My Song

Song of the Sky Loom / Hunting Song

Teaching Options (from Teacher's Edition)

Mini Lessons

Vocabulary Strategy
____ Using Context Clues   ❏ Vocabulary Transparencies and Copymasters, C18

Grammar
____ Forming and Distinguishing Plurals from   ❏ Grammar Transparencies and Copymasters, C64
Possessives

Viewing and Representing
Art Appreciation
____ *Born Free* by Edwin Salomon

Assessment
____ Selection Test   ❏ Formal Assessment: Selection Test, p. 9
____ Test Generator

Homework Assignments

_____

_____

_____

_____

_____

Other Teaching Materials

_____

_____

_____

_____

Coyote Stories

Core Objectives
- Understand and appreciate trickster tales
- Use strategies for reading trickster tales

Integrating Skills

Grammar	Vocabulary
■ Capitalization	■ Context Clues
■ Different Types of Sentences	■ Expanding Vocabulary Through Wide Reading

> **MISSOURI PLANNER**
> Grade-Level Expectations
> R1.C, R1.D, R1.F, R1.G, R1.H, R1.I, R2.A, R2.C, IL2.A

Preparing to Read
____ Connect to Your Life
____ Build Background
____ Focus Your Reading
      Literary Analysis: Trickster Tales   ❏ Unit One Resource Book: Literary Analysis SkillBuilder, p. 18
      Active Reading: Strategies for Reading   ❏ Unit One Resource Book: Active Reading SkillBuilder, p. 17
        Trickster Tales

Teaching the Literature
____ Reading the Selection   ❏ PE pp. 39–47
                                      ❏ Unit One Resource Book: Summary, pp. 15–16

Thinking Through the Literature
____ Connect to the Literature
____ Think Critically   ❏ Reading and Critical Thinking Transparencies, T15, T48
____ Extend Interpretations
____ Literary Analysis: Trickster Tales   ❏ Literary Analysis Transparencies, T24

Choices and Challenges

Writing Options
____ Magazine Article
____ Updated Trickster Tale

Activities and Explorations
____ Creating Pantomime
____ Coyote on Video

Coyote Stories

Teaching Options (from Teacher's Edition)

Mini Lessons

Vocabulary Strategy

____ Using Context Clues and Footnotes

____ Expanding Vocabulary Through Wide
Reading
    ❏ Vocabulary Transparencies and Copymasters, C19

Grammar

____ Capitalization of Proper Nouns and
Adjectives
    ❏ Grammar Transparencies and Copymasters, C142

____ Identifying Different Types of Sentences
    ❏ Grammar Transparencies and Copymasters, C74

Viewing and Representing

Art Appreciation

____ *Nootka Wood Whale Effigy Rattle*
by anonymous

____ *Mask for a Coyote Dance* by anonymous

Informal Assessment

____ Arrange Events in Sequential Order

Assessment

____ Selection Quiz   ❏ Unit One Resource Book: Selection Quiz, p. 19

____ Selection Test   ❏ Formal Assessment: Selection Test, pp. 11–12

____ Test Generator

Homework Assignments	Other Teaching Materials

The Man to Send Rain Clouds

Core Objectives
- Understand and appreciate a short story
- Recognize author's use of conflict
- Make inferences based on information presented in a story

> **MISSOURI PLANNER**
> Grade-Level Expectations
> R1.C, R1.D, R1.F, R1.G, R1.H, R1.I, R2.A, R2.C, W1.A, W3.C

Integrating Skills

Grammar
- Capitalizing First Word of a Sentence

Vocabulary
- Context Clues

Preparing to Read
____ Comparing Literature
____ Build Background
____ Vocabulary Preview: Context Clues   ❏ Unit One Resource Book: Words to Know SkillBuilder, p. 23
____ Focus Your Reading
     Literary Analysis: Conflict   ❏ Unit One Resource Book: Literary Analysis SkillBuilder, p. 22
     Active Reading: Making Inferences   ❏ Unit One Resource Book: Active Reading SkillBuilder, p. 21

Teaching the Literature
        ❏ PE pp. 48–54
____ Reading the Selection   ❏ Unit One Resource Book: Summary, p. 20

Thinking Through the Literature
____ Connect to the Literature
____ Think Critically   ❏ Reading and Critical Thinking Transparencies, T7
____ Extend Interpretations
____ Literary Analysis: Conflict   ❏ Literary Analysis Transparencies, T14

Choices and Challenges

Writing Options
____ Performance Review
____ Descriptions of Rites

Activities and Explorations
____ Illustrative Scene
____ Points of Comparison

Vocabulary in Action
____ Related Words

Author Activity
____ Silko the Storyteller

The Man to Send Rain Clouds

Teaching Options (from Teacher's Edition)

Mini Lessons

Preteaching Vocabulary
____ Context Clues

Grammar
____ Capitalizing First Word of Sentence   ❑ Grammar Transparencies and Copymasters, C146

Viewing and Representing
Art Appreciation
____ *Between Heaven and Earth; Earth and Sky*
by Frank LaPena

Cross Curricular Link

History
____ Laguna Pueblo

Informal Assessment

____ Identifying Implied Main Idea

Assessment

____ Selection Quiz   ❑ Unit One Resource Book: Selection Quiz, p. 24
____ Selection Test   ❑ Formal Assessment: Selection Test, pp. 13–14
____ Test Generator

Homework Assignments

_____

_____

_____

_____

_____

Other Teaching Materials

_____

_____

_____

_____

_____

Selection Lesson Plan   *Name* _____   *Date* _____

The Way to Rainy Mountain

Pages 55–63

Core Objectives
- Understand and appreciate a personal narrative
- Appreciate author's use of setting
- Understand the structure of a personal narrative

> **MISSOURI PLANNER**
> Grade-Level Expectations
> R1.C, R1.D, R1.F, R1.G, R1.H, R1.I, R2.A, R2.C, W1.A

Integrating Skills

Grammar	Vocabulary
■ Pronouns	■ Using Reference Materials
■ Predicates	■ Connotations

Preparing to Read
____ Comparing Literature
____ Build Background
____ Vocabulary Preview: Using Reference Materials   ❑ Unit One Resource Book: Words to Know SkillBuilder, p. 28
____ Focus Your Reading
       Literary Analysis: Setting   ❑ Unit One Resource Book: Literary Analysis SkillBuilder, p. 27
       Active Reading: Understanding Structure   ❑ Unit One Resource Book: Active Reading SkillBuilder, p. 26

Teaching the Literature
❑ PE pp. 55–63
____ Reading the Selection   ❑ Unit One Resource Book: Summary, p. 25

Thinking Through the Literature
____ Connect to the Literature
____ Think Critically   ❑ Reading and Critical Thinking Transparencies, T6, T17
____ Extend Interpretations
____ Literary Analysis: Setting   ❑ Literary Analysis Transparencies, T13

Choices and Challenges
Writing Options
____ A Fitting Eulogy
____ Points of Comparison

Activities and Explorations
____ Points of Comparison

Vocabulary in Action
____ Assessment Practice

The Way to Rainy Mountain

Teaching Options (from Teacher's Edition)

Mini Lessons

Preteaching Vocabulary
____ Using Reference Materials

Vocabulary Strategy
____ Interpreting Connotations   ❑ Vocabulary Transparencies and Copymasters, C26

Grammar
____ Pronouns   ❑ Grammar Transparencies and Copymasters, C65
____ Compound and Simple Predicates   ❑ Grammar Transparencies and Copymasters, C77

Speaking and Listening
____ Presenting Interpretations

Cross Curricular Link

Science
____ The Roots of the Plains

Informal Assessment
____ Arranging Events in Sequential Order

Assessment

____ Selection Quiz   ❑ Unit One Resource Book: Selection Quiz, p. 29
____ Selection Test   ❑ Formal Assessment: Selection Test, pp. 15–16
____ Part Test   ❑ Formal Assessment: Unit One, Part 1 Test, pp. 17–18
____ Test Generator

Homework Assignments

_____

_____

_____

_____

_____

Other Teaching Materials

_____

_____

_____

_____

_____

from La Relación

Core Objectives
- Read a nonfiction report
- Examine how audience influences the author
- Use text organizers

MISSOURI PLANNER
Grade-Level Expectations
R1.C, R1.D, R1.E, R1.F, R1.G, R1.H, R1.I, R2.A, R2.C, W1.A, W3.C, IL1.A, IL1.B, IL1.C

Integrating Skills

Grammar
- Simple Sentences
- Review Parts of Speech

Vocabulary
- Using Context Clues
- Applying Prefix and Root Word Meanings

Preparing to Read
____ Connect to Your Life
____ Build Background
____ Vocabulary Preview: Using Context Clues   ❑ Unit One Resource Book: Words to Know SkillBuilder, p. 34
____ Focus Your Reading
Literary Analysis: Audience   ❑ Unit One Resource Book: Literary Analysis SkillBuilder, p. 33
Active Reading: Using Text Organizers   ❑ Unit One Resource Book: Active Reading SkillBuilder, p. 32

Teaching the Literature
____ Reading the Selection
❑ PE pp. 72–80
❑ Unit One Resource Book: Summary, p. 31

Thinking Through the Literature
____ Connect to the Literature
____ Think Critically   ❑ Reading and Critical Thinking Transparencies, T16, T37
____ Extend Interpretations
____ Literary Analysis: Audience   ❑ Literary Analysis Transparencies, T1

Choices and Challenges

Writing Options
____ Firsthand Account
____ Essay on Leadership
____ Report to the President

Activities and Explorations
____ Miniseries Storyboard
____ Karankawa Speech
____ Informal Debate
____ Bar Graph

Inquiry and Research
____ Early Explorers

Art Connection
____ History Through Art

---

from La Relación

Choices and Challenges (continued)

Vocabulary in Action
____ Context Clues

Author Activity
____ Just Like Fiction

Teaching Options (from Teacher's Edition)

Mini Lessons

Preteaching Vocabulary
____ Using Context Clues

Vocabulary Strategy
____ Applying Prefix and Root Word Meanings   ❑ Vocabulary Transparencies and Copymasters, C27

Grammar
____ Simple Sentences: Subject, Predicate   ❑ Grammar Transparencies and Copymasters, C75
____ Review: Parts of Speech   ❑ Grammar Transparencies and Copymasters, C62

Speaking and Listening
____ Dramatic Reading and Retelling

Informal Assessment
____ Character Empathy

Assessment
____ Selection Quiz   ❑ Unit One Resource Book: Selection Quiz, p. 35
____ Selection Test   ❑ Formal Assessment: Selection Test, pp. 19–20
____ Test Generator

Homework Assignments

_____
_____
_____
_____
_____

Other Teaching Materials

_____
_____
_____
_____
_____

from Of Plymouth Plantation

Core Objectives
- Understand and appreciate a historical chronicle
- Examine primary sources
- Summarize text by identifying main ideas and supporting details

```
┌─────────────────────────────────┐
│        MISSOURI PLANNER          │
│     Grade-Level Expectations     │
│ R1.C, R1.D, R1.F, R1.G, R1.H, R1.I, R2.A, │
│ R2.C, W1.A, W3.C, IL1.A, IL1.B, IL1.C │
└─────────────────────────────────┘
```

Integrating Skills

Grammar
- Sentence Fragments
- Run-on Sentences

Vocabulary
- Using Context Clues
- Researching Word Origins

Preparing to Read
____ Connect to Your Life
____ Build Background
____ Vocabulary Preview: Using Context Clues ☐ Unit One Resource Book: Words to Know SkillBuilder, p. 39
____ Focus Your Reading

Literary Analysis: Primary Sources ☐ Unit One Resource Book: Literary Analysis SkillBuilder, p. 38
Active Reading: Summarizing ☐ Unit One Resource Book: Active Reading SkillBuilder, p. 37

Teaching the Literature
____ Reading the Selection
☐ PE pp. 81–90
☐ Unit One Resource Book: Summary, p. 36

Thinking Through the Literature
____ Connect to the Literature
____ Think Critically ☐ Reading and Critical Thinking Transparencies, T10, T19, T22
____ Extend Interpretations
____ Literary Analysis: Primary Sources ☐ Literary Analysis Transparencies, T1, T2

Choices and Challenges

Writing Options
____ Squanto's Diary
____ Eyewitness Account
____ Interview Questions

Activities and Explorations
____ Pilgrim Memorial
____ Musical Soundtrack
____ Time Line

Inquiry and Research
____ The Voyage of the Pilgrims

Art Connection
____ Illustration of Plymouth Colony

Vocabulary in Action
____ Meaning Clues

Selection Lesson Plan (continued)
from Of Plymouth Plantation

Choices and Challenges (continued)
Author Activity
___ Profiles in Courage

Teaching Options (from Teacher's Edition)
Mini Lessons
Preteaching Vocabulary
___ Using Context Clues

Vocabulary Strategy
___ Researching Word Origins   ❑ Vocabulary Transparencies and Copymasters, C22

Grammar
___ Sentence Fragments   ❑ Grammar Transparencies and Copymasters, C107
___ Run-on Sentences   ❑ Grammar Transparencies and Copymasters, C109

Speaking and Listening
___ Oral History

Viewing and Representing
Art Appreciation
___ *View of Plymouth, 1627* by Cal Sachs

Cross Curricular Link
Social Studies
___ Squanto

Informal Assessment
___ Parallel Account

Assessment
___ Selection Quiz   ❑ Unit One Resource Book: Selection Quiz, p. 40
___ Selection Test   ❑ Formal Assessment: Selection Test, pp. 21–22
___ Test Generator

Homework Assignments
_____
_____
_____
_____
_____

Other Teaching Materials
_____
_____
_____
_____
_____

from The Interesting Narrative of the Life of Olaudah Equiano

Pages 93–99

Core Objectives
- Understand and appreciate a slave narrative
- Analyze details

MISSOURI PLANNER

Grade-Level Expectations

R1.C, R1.D, R1.F, R1.G, R1.H, R1.I, R2.A, R2.C, W1.A, W3.C

Integrating Skills

Grammar
- Structure: Compound Sentences

Vocabulary
- Using Context Clues and Reference Materials

Preparing to Read
____ Connect to Your Life
____ Build Background
____ Vocabulary Preview: Using Context Clues and Reference Materials   ❑ Unit One Resource Book: Words to Know SkillBuilder, p. 44
____ Focus Your Reading
   Literary Analysis: Slave Narratives   ❑ Unit One Resource Book: Literary Analysis SkillBuilder, p. 43
   Active Reading: Analyzing Details   ❑ Unit One Resource Book: Active Reading SkillBuilder, p. 42

Teaching the Literature
____ Reading the Selection

❑ PE pp. 93–99
❑ Unit One Resource Book: Summary, p. 41

Thinking Through the Literature
____ Connect to the Literature
____ Think Critically   ❑ Reading and Critical Thinking Transparencies, T10, T46
____ Extend Interpretations
____ Literary Analysis: Slave Narratives   ❑ Literary Analysis Transparencies, T1, T2

Choices and Challenges

Writing Options
____ Song of Freedom
____ Narrative Summary

Activities and Explorations
____ Museum Exhibit

Vocabulary in Action
____ Assessment Practice

Author Activity
____ Personal and Political

from The Interesting Narrative of the Life of Olaudah Equiano

Teaching Options (from Teacher's Edition)

Mini Lessons

Preteaching Vocabulary
____ Using Context Clues and Reference Materials

Vocabulary Strategy
____ Using Context Clues and Reference Materials

Grammar
____ Structure: Compound Sentences   ❏ Grammar Transparencies and Copymasters, C110

Viewing and Representing
Art Appreciation
____ *The Slave Ship* (detail) by Robert Riggs

Cross Curricular Link

History
____ Slavery

Informal Assessment

____ Open-Ended Test Questions

Assessment

____ Selection Quiz   ❏ Unit One Resource Book: Selection Quiz, p. 45
____ Selection Test   ❏ Formal Assessment: Selection Test, pp. 23–24
____ Test Generator

Homework Assignments

_____
_____
_____
_____
_____

Other Teaching Materials

_____
_____
_____
_____
_____

from Blue Highways

Core Objectives
- Appreciate a travelogue
- Examine author's purpose
- Organize details

<table>
<tr><td colspan="2" align="center">**MISSOURI PLANNER**</td></tr>
<tr><td colspan="2" align="center">Grade-Level Expectations</td></tr>
<tr><td colspan="2">R1.C, R1.D, R1.F, R1.G, R1.H, R1.I, R2.A, R2.C, W1.A, W3.C</td></tr>
</table>

Integrating Skills

Grammar
- Complex Sentences
- Pronouns

Vocabulary
- Context Clues
- Prefixes, Suffixes, and Root Words

Preparing to Read
____ Comparing Literature
____ Build Background
____ Vocabulary Preview: Context Clues   ❏ Unit One Resource Book: Words to Know SkillBuilder, p. 49
____ Focus Your Reading
      Literary Analysis: Author's Purpose   ❏ Unit One Resource Book: Literary Analysis SkillBuilder, p. 48
      Active Reading: Organizing Details   ❏ Unit One Resource Book: Active Reading SkillBuilder, p. 47

Teaching the Literature
❏ PE pp. 100–108
____ Reading the Selection   ❏ Unit One Resource Book: Summary, p. 46

Thinking Through the Literature
____ Connect to the Literature
____ Think Critically   ❏ Reading and Critical Thinking Transparencies, T19, T48, T55
____ Extend Interpretations
____ Literary Analysis: Author's Purpose   ❏ Literary Analysis Transparencies, T16

Choices and Challenges
Writing Options
____ Hopi Dialogue
____ Personal Essay on Beliefs
____ Points of Comparison

Vocabulary in Action
____ Related Words

from Blue Highways

Teaching Options (from Teacher's Edition)

Mini Lessons

Preteaching Vocabulary
____ Context Clues

Vocabulary Strategy
____ Prefixes, Suffixes, and Root Words

Grammar
____ Complex Sentences   ❑ Grammar Transparencies and Copymasters, C111
____ Pronouns   ❑ Grammar Transparencies and Copymasters, C125

Viewing and Representing
Art Appreciation
____ *Road Past the View* by Georgia O'Keefe

Cross Curricular Link

History
____ The Indian Citizenship Act of 1924

Informal Assessment
____ Distinguishing Between Fact and Nonfact

Assessment
____ Selection Quiz   ❑ Unit One Resource Book: Selection Quiz, p. 50
____ Selection Test   ❑ Formal Assessment: Selection Test, pp. 25–26
____ Test Generator

Homework Assignments

_____

_____

_____

_____

_____

Other Teaching Materials

_____

_____

_____

_____

_____

My Sojourn in the Lands of My Ancestors

Core Objectives
- Understand and appreciate an autobiography
- Apply strategies for reading autobiography

Integrating Skills

MISSOURI PLANNER
Grade-Level Expectations
R1.C, R1.D, R1.F, R1.G, R1.H, R1.I, R2.A, R2.C, W1.A, W3.C

Grammar
- Compound-Complex Sentences

Vocabulary
- Using Context Clues and Reference Materials

Preparing to Read
____ Comparing Literature
____ Build Background
____ Vocabulary Preview: Using Context Clues and Reference Materials   ❑ Unit One Resource Book: Words to Know SkillBuilder, p. 54
____ Focus Your Reading
     Literary Analysis: Autobiography   ❑ Unit One Resource Book: Literary Analysis SkillBuilder, p. 53
     Active Reading: Strategies for Reading   ❑ Unit One Resource Book: Active Reading SkillBuilder, p. 52
     Autobiography

Teaching the Literature
____ Reading the Selection   ❑ PE pp. 109–117
                                  ❑ Unit One Resource Book: Summary, p. 51

Thinking Through the Literature
____ Connect to the Literature
____ Think Critically
____ Extend Interpretations
____ Literary Analysis: Autobiography

Choices and Challenges
Writing Options
____ Description of Place
____ Poetry of Experience
____ Points of Comparison

Vocabulary in Action
____ Meaning Clues

My Sojourn in the Lands of My Ancestors

Teaching Options (from Teacher's Edition)

Mini Lessons

Preteaching Vocabulary
____ Using Context Clues and Reference Materials

Speaking and Listening
____ Poetry Reading

Grammar
____ Compound-Complex Sentences

Cross Curricular Link

History
____ Manhattan's African Burial Ground

Informal Assessment
____ Choosing the Best Summary

Assessment

____ Selection Quiz
____ Selection Test
____ Part Test
____ Test Generator

❑ Unit One Resource Book: Selection Quiz, p. 55
❑ Formal Assessment: Selection Test, pp. 27–28
❑ Formal Assessment: Unit One, Part 2 Test, pp. 29–30

Homework Assignments

_____
_____
_____
_____
_____

Other Teaching Materials

_____
_____
_____
_____

Eyewitness Report

Writing Prompt

Write an eyewitness report describing an event
that has personal or historical significance.

MISSOURI PLANNER
Grade-Level Expectations
R3.D, W1.A, W2.E, W3.A, W3.C

Preparing to Read

____ Introduction

____ Basics in a Box

____ Using the Graphic

❑ Writing Transparencies and Copymasters, T11, T20, C25

____ Analyzing a Student Model
"Far from the Land of Opportunity"

❑ Unit One Resource Book: Student Models, pp. 62–67

Writing

____ **Prewriting**
Choosing a Subject
Planning the Eyewitness Report

❑ Unit One Resource Book: Prewriting, p. 57

____ **Drafting**
Organizing the Draft

❑ Unit One Resource Book: Drafting and Elaboration, p. 58

____ **Peer Review**
Ask Your Peer Reader

❑ Unit One Resource Book: Peer Response Guide, pp. 59–60

____ **Revising**
Elaborating with Sensory Details

❑ Unit One Resource Book: Revising, Editing, and Proofreading, p. 61
❑ Unit One Resource Book: Rubric for Evaluation, p. 68

____ **Editing and Proofreading**
Modifier Placement

____ **Reflecting**

Homework Assignments

_____
_____
_____
_____
_____

Other Teaching Materials

_____
_____
_____
_____
_____

To My Dear and Loving Husband / Upon the Burning of Our House, July 10th, 1666

Pages 138–143

Core Objectives
- Understand and appreciate lyric poetry
- Appreciate author's use of meter
- Clarify meaning of archaic language

> **MISSOURI PLANNER**
> Grade-Level Expectations
> R1.C, R1.D, R1.F, R1.G, R1.H, R1.I, R2.A, R2.C, W1.A, IL1.A, IL1.B, IL1.C

Integrating Skills

Grammar	Vocabulary
■ Auxiliary Verbs	■ Analogies

Preparing to Read
____ Connect to Your Life
____ Build Background
____ Focus Your Reading
    Literary Analysis: Meter   ❑ Unit Two Resource Book: Literary Analysis SkillBuilder, p. 5
    Active Reading: Clarifying Meaning   ❑ Unit Two Resource Book: Active Reading SkillBuilder, p. 4

Teaching the Literature
____ Reading the Selection   ❑ PE pp. 138–143

Thinking Through the Literature
____ Connect to the Literature
____ Think Critically   ❑ Reading and Critical Thinking Transparencies, T15, T26
____ Extend Interpretations
____ Literary Analysis: Meter   ❑ Literary Analysis Transparencies, T11

Choices and Challenges
Writing Options
____ Lyric Poem
____ Personal Analogy

Activities and Explorations
____ Storyboard Illustrations
____ Musical Adaptation

Inquiry and Research
____ Puritan Women
____ Puritan Homes

To My Dear and Loving Husband / Upon the Burning of Our House, July 10th, 1666

Teaching Options (from Teacher's Edition)

Mini Lessons

Vocabulary Strategy
___ Reading and Understanding Analogies   ❏ Vocabulary Transparencies and Copymasters, C24

Grammar
___ Auxiliary Verbs   ❏ Grammar Transparencies and Copymasters, C67

Informal Assessment
___ Journal Entry

Assessment
___ Selection Test   ❏ Formal Assessment: Selection Test, pp. 31–32
___ Test Generator

Homework Assignments

_____
_____
_____
_____
_____

Other Teaching Materials

_____
_____
_____
_____
_____

The Examination of Sarah Good

Pages 144–149

Core Objectives
- Understand and appreciate a court transcript
- Detect bias in a speaker's language

MISSOURI PLANNER
Grade-Level Expectations
R1.C, R1.D, R1.F, R1.G, R1.H, R1.I, R2.A, R2.C, W1.A, W3.C, IL1.A, IL1.B, IL1.C

Integrating Skills

Grammar
- Overuse of the Verb *To Be*

Vocabulary
- Idioms

Preparing to Read
____ Connect to Your Life
____ Build Background
____ Focus Your Reading
     Literary Analysis: Transcript
     Active Reading: Detecting Bias
     Active Reading: Distinguishing Fact from Opinion

❑ Unit Two Resource Book: Literary Analysis SkillBuilder, p. 8
❑ Unit Two Resource Book: Active Reading SkillBuilder, p. 7

Teaching the Literature
____ Reading the Selection

❑ PE pp. 144–149
❑ Unit Two Resource Book: Summary, p. 6

Thinking Through the Literature
____ Connect to the Literature
____ Think Critically
____ Extend Interpretations
____ Literary Analysis: Transcript

❑ Reading and Critical Thinking Transparencies, T22

Choices and Challenges

Writing Options
____ Courtroom Drama
____ Plea for Mercy
____ Explanation of Motives

Activities and Explorations
____ Courtroom Sketches
____ Media Coverage
____ Legal Discussion

Inquiry and Research
____ Salem Witch Trials
____ Salem Memorials

Art Connection
____ Mental Picture

The Examination of Sarah Good

Teaching Options (from Teacher's Edition)

Mini Lessons

Vocabulary Strategy
____ Using Context to Determine the Meaning   ❑ Vocabulary Transparencies and Copymasters, C25
of Idioms

Grammar
____ Overuse of the Verb *To Be*   ❑ Grammar Transparencies and Copymasters, C163

Informal Assessment
____ Understanding Multiple-Meaning Words

Assessment
____ Selection Quiz   ❑ Unit Two Resource Book: Selection Quiz, p. 9
____ Selection Test   ❑ Formal Assessment: Selection Test, pp. 33–34
____ Test Generator

Homework Assignments

_____

_____

_____

_____

_____

Other Teaching Materials

_____

_____

_____

_____

_____

from Sinners in the Hands of an Angry God   Pages 152–160

Core Objectives
- Analyze an 18th-century sermon
- Appreciate author's use of persuasive writing
- Analyze emotional language

MISSOURI PLANNER

Grade-Level Expectations

R1.C, R1.D, R1.F, R1.G, R1.H, R1.I, R2.A, R2.C, W1.A, W3.C

Integrating Skills

Grammar
- Subject-Verb Agreement

Vocabulary
- Context Clues
- Connotation

Preparing to Read
____ Connect to Your Life
____ Build Background
____ Vocabulary Preview: Using Context Clues   ❑ Unit Two Resource Book: Words to Know SkillBuilder, p. 13
____ Focus Your Reading
      Literary Analysis: Persuasive Writing   ❑ Unit Two Resource Book: Literary Analysis SkillBuilder, p. 12
      Active Reading: Analyzing Emotional Language   ❑ Unit Two Resource Book: Active Reading SkillBuilder, p. 11

Teaching the Literature
       ❑ PE pp. 152–160
____ Reading the Selection   ❑ Unit Two Resource Book: Summary, p. 10

Thinking Through the Literature
____ Connect to the Literature
____ Think Critically   ❑ Reading and Critical Thinking Transparencies, T15, T18
____ Extend Interpretations
____ Literary Analysis: Persuasive Writing   ❑ Literary Analysis Transparencies, T9

Choices and Challenges

Writing Options
____ Letter of Opinion
____ Vivid Comparison
____ Public Service Announcement

Activities and Explorations
____ Live Performance
____ Jacket Cover

Inquiry and Research
____ Inspirational Speakers
____ Artistic Visions

Vocabulary in Action
____ Assessment Practice

Author Activity
____ A Vision of Terror and Beauty

from Sinners in the Hands of an Angry God

Teaching Options (from Teacher's Edition)

Mini Lessons

Preteaching Vocabulary
____ Using Context Clues

Vocabulary Strategy
____ Interpreting the Connotative Power of Words   ❑ Vocabulary Transparencies and Copymasters, C26

Grammar
____ Subject-Verb Agreement   ❑ Grammar Transparencies and Copymasters, C123

Viewing and Representing
Art Appreciation
____ *Un quadro di fuochi preziosi* [*A painting of precious fires*] by Enzo Cucchi

Cross Curricular Link

History
____ Puritan Intolerance

Informal Assessment
____ Choosing the Best Summary

Assessment

____ Selection Quiz   ❑ Unit Two Resource Book: Selection Quiz, p. 14
____ Selection Test   ❑ Formal Assessment: Selection Test, pp. 35–36
____ Test Generator

Homework Assignments

_____
_____
_____
_____
_____

Other Teaching Materials

_____
_____
_____
_____
_____

The Crucible, Act One

Core Objectives
- Understand and appreciate a drama
- Understand author's use of stage directions
- Use a graphic organizer to keep track of details in a play

> **MISSOURI PLANNER**
> Grade-Level Expectations
> R1.C, R1.D, R1.F, R1.G, R1.H, R1.I, R2.A, R2.C

Integrating Skills

Grammar
- Interjections
- Regular and Irregular Verbs
- Principal Parts of Verbs
- Perfect Tenses

Vocabulary
- Using Reference Materials
- Prefixes and Root Words
- Context Clues
- Multiple-Meaning Words
- Word Origins

Preparing to Read

____ Comparing Literature
____ Build Background
____ Vocabulary Preview: Using Reference Materials
____ Focus Your Reading
     Literary Analysis: Stage Directions
     Active Reading: Using a Graphic Organizer

❑ Unit Two Resource Book: Words to Know SkillBuilder, p. 18, p. 23, p. 28, p. 33

❑ Unit Two Resource Book: Literary Analysis SkillBuilder, p. 17, p. 22, p. 27, p. 32

❑ Unit Two Resource Book: Active Reading SkillBuilder, p. 16, p. 21, p. 26, p. 31

Teaching the Literature

____ Reading the Selection

❑ PE pp. 163–190
❑ Unit Two Resource Book: Summary, p. 15

Thinking Through the Literature

____ Connect to the Literature
____ Think Critically
____ Extend Interpretations
____ Literary Analysis: Stage Directions

❑ Reading and Critical Thinking Transparencies, T6, T15, T52

❑ Literary Analysis Transparencies, T3, T4, T5

The Crucible, Act One

Teaching Options (from Teacher's Edition)

Mini Lessons

Preteaching Vocabulary
____ Using Reference Materials

Vocabulary Strategy
____ Applying Meanings of Prefixes and Root Words   ❑ Vocabulary Transparencies and Copymasters, C27

Grammar
____ Interjections   ❑ Grammar Transparencies and Copymasters, C72
____ Regular and Irregular Verbs   ❑ Grammar Transparencies and Copymasters, C113

Viewing and Representing
____ Photograph

Cross Curricular Link

History
____ Barbados

Informal Assessment
____ Recognizing Facts and Details
____ Making Inferences and Drawing Conclusions
____ Alternative Ending

Assessment
____ Selection Quiz   ❑ Unit Two Resource Book: Selection Quiz, p. 19
____ Selection Test   ❑ Formal Assessment: Selection Test, pp. 37–38
____ Test Generator

Homework Assignments

_____
_____
_____
_____
_____

Other Teaching Materials

_____
_____
_____
_____

The Crucible, Act Two

Core Objectives
See page 29.

```
┌─────────────────────────────────────────┐
│           MISSOURI PLANNER                │
│        Grade-Level Expectations           │
│ R1.C, R1.D, R1.F, R1.G, R1.H, R1.I, R2.A, R2.C │
└─────────────────────────────────────────┘
```

Integrating Skills

Grammar
■ Principal Parts of
   Verbs

Vocabulary
■ Using Context Clues
■ Applying Prefixes and Root
   Words

Teaching the Literature
____ Reading the Selection

❑ PE pp. 191–206
❑ Unit Two Resource Book: Summary, p. 20

Thinking Through the Literature
____ Connect to the Literature
____ Think Critically
____ Extend Interpretations
____ Literary Analysis: Dialogue

❑ Reading and Critical Thinking Transparencies, T6, T15, T52

❑ Literary Analysis Transparencies, T3, T4, T5

Teaching Options (from Teacher's Edition)

Mini Lessons

Vocabulary Strategy
____ Using Context Clues
____ Applying Prefixes and Root Words

❑ Vocabulary Transparencies and Copymasters, C27

Grammar
____ Principal Parts of Verbs

❑ Grammar Transparencies and Copymasters, C114

Viewing and Representing
____ Photograph

Cross Curricular Link

History
____ McCarthy Hearings

Informal Assessment
____ Arranging Events in Sequential Order
____ Perceiving Cause and Effect Relationships

The Crucible, Act Two

Assessment

____ Selection Quiz

____ Selection Test

____ Test Generator

❑ Unit Two Resource Book: Selection Quiz, p. 24

❑ Formal Assessment: Selection Test, pp. 39–40

Homework Assignments	Other Teaching Materials

The Crucible, Act Three

Core Objectives
See page 29.

> **MISSOURI PLANNER**
> Grade-Level Expectations
> R1.C, R1.D, R1.F, R1.G, R1.H, R1.I, R2.A, R2.C

Integrating Skills

Grammar
- Perfect Tenses

Vocabulary
- Using Context Clues
- Understanding Multiple-Meaning Words

Teaching the Literature
____ Reading the Selection

- ❑ PE pp. 207–228
- ❑ Unit Two Resource Book: Summary, p. 25

Thinking Through the Literature
____ Connect to the Literature
____ Think Critically
____ Extend Interpretations
____ Literary Analysis: Foil

- ❑ Reading and Critical Thinking Transparencies, T6, T15, T52
- ❑ Literary Analysis Transparencies, T3, T4, T5

Teaching Options (from Teacher's Edition)

Mini Lessons

Vocabulary Strategy
____ Using Context Clues
____ Understanding Multiple-Meaning Words

Grammar
____ Perfect Tenses

- ❑ Grammar Transparencies and Copymasters, C115

Speaking and Listening
____ Role-Playing

Cross Curricular Links

History
____ Witchcraft Trials

Logic
____ Inductive and Deductive Reasoning

Psychology
____ Hysteria

Informal Assessment
____ Court Reporter
____ Predicting Probable Future Actions
____ Describing Character

The Crucible, Act Three

Assessment
____ Selection Quiz
____ Selection Test
____ Test Generator

❑ Unit Two Resource Book: Selection Quiz, p. 29
❑ Formal Assessment: Selection Test, pp. 41–42

Homework Assignments

_____

_____

_____

_____

_____

Other Teaching Materials

_____

_____

_____

_____

The Crucible, Act Four

Core Objectives
See page 29.

```
┌─────────────────────────────────────────┐
│            MISSOURI PLANNER               │
│         Grade-Level Expectations          │
│  R1.C, R1.D, R1.F, R1.G, R1.H, R1.I, R2.A, R2.C,  │
│  W1.A, W3.C, IL1.A, IL1.B, IL1.C          │
└─────────────────────────────────────────┘
```

Integrating Skills
Vocabulary
- Using Context Clues
- Researching Word Origins

Teaching the Literature
____ Reading the Selection

❏ PE pp. 229–245
❏ Unit Two Resource Book: Summary, p. 30

Thinking Through the Literature
____ Connect to the Literature
____ Think Critically
____ Extend Interpretations
____ Literary Analysis: Plot and Conflict

❏ Reading and Critical Thinking Transparencies, T6, T15, T52

❏ Literary Analysis Transparencies, T3, T4, T5

Choices and Challenges
Writing Options
____ Points of Comparison
____ Missing Scene
____ Editorial on Hysteria
____ Capsule Review

Activities and Explorations
____ Historical Fashions
____ Set Design
____ Dramatic Reading
____ Salem Game Show

Inquiry and Research
____ History vs. Drama
____ McCarthyism

Vocabulary in Action
____ Context Clues
____ Assessment Practice

Teaching Options (from Teacher's Edition)

Mini Lessons

Vocabulary Strategy
____ Using Context Clues
____ Researching Word Origins

Speaking and Listening
____ Staging a Mock Trial
____ Performing the Climactic Scene

Viewing and Representing
____ Darkness and Light

Cross Curricular Link

Workplace
____ Communicating

Informal Assessment
____ Making Inferences
____ Alternative Ending

Assessment
____ Selection Quiz
____ Selection Test
____ Part Test

❏ Unit Two Resource Book: Selection Quiz, p. 34
❏ Formal Assessment: Selection Test, pp. 43–44
❏ Formal Assessment: Unit Two: Part 1 Test, pp. 45–46

Homework Assignments
_____
_____
_____
_____
_____

Other Teaching Materials
_____
_____
_____
_____
_____

Critical Review

Writing Prompt

Write a review of a piece of literature or a film
you feel strongly about. You will establish
evaluation criteria and express your opinion
of the piece.

Preparing to Read

____ Introduction
____ Basics in a Box
____ Using the Graphic

❑ Writing Transparencies and Copymasters, T11, T20, C26

____ Analyzing a Professional Model
"Movie Review of *The Crucible*"

❑ Unit Two Resource Book: Student Models, pp. 41–46

Writing

____ **Prewriting**
Choosing a Subject
Planning the Critical Review

❑ Unit Two Resource Book: Prewriting, p. 36

____ **Drafting**
Organizing the Draft

❑ Unit Two Resource Book: Drafting and Elaboration, p. 37

____ **Peer Review**
Ask Your Peer Reader

❑ Unit Two Resource Book: Peer Response Guide, pp. 38–39

____ **Revising**
Avoiding Circular Reasoning

❑ Unit Two Resource Book: Revising, Editing, and Proofreading, p. 40
❑ Unit Two Resource Book: Rubric for Evaluation, p. 47

____ **Editing and Proofreading**
Eliminating Qualifiers

____ **Reflecting**

Homework Assignments

_____
_____
_____
_____
_____

Other Teaching Materials

_____
_____
_____
_____
_____

Speech in the Virginia Convention

Core Objectives
- Understand a persuasive speech
- Appreciate use of allusion
- Analyze the use of rhetorical questions and persuasion

> **MISSOURI PLANNER**
> Grade-Level Expectations
> R1.C, R1.D, R1.F, R1.G, R1.H, R1.I, R2.A, R2.C, W1.A, LS2.A, IL1.A, IL1.B, IL1.C

Integrating Skills

Grammar
- Perfect Tenses

Vocabulary
- Context Clues

Preparing to Read
____ Connect to Your Life
____ Build Background
____ Vocabulary Preview: Using Context Clues   ❏ Unit Two Resource Book: Words to Know SkillBuilder, p. 53
____ Focus Your Reading
       Literary Analysis: Allusion   ❏ Unit Two Resource Book: Literary Analysis SkillBuilder, p. 52
       Active Reading: Rhetorical Questions and   ❏ Unit Two Resource Book: Active Reading SkillBuilder, p. 51
          Persuasion

Teaching the Literature
                                                       ❏ PE pp. 262–269
____ Reading the Selection   ❏ Unit Two Resource Book: Summary, p. 50

Thinking Through the Literature
____ Connect to the Literature
____ Think Critically   ❏ Reading and Critical Thinking Transparencies, T20, T21
____ Extend Interpretations
____ Literary Analysis: Allusion   ❏ Literary Analysis Transparencies, T9

Choices and Challenges

Writing Options
____ Newspaper Report
____ Character Sketch
____ Rebuttal Speech

Activities and Explorations
____ Political Advertisement
____ Liberty Poster
____ Dramatic Reading
____ Independence Discussion

____ **Art Connection**

Inquiry and Research
____ Countdown to Revolution

Vocabulary in Action
____ Classifying Words

Speech in the Virginia Convention

Teaching Options (from Teacher's Edition)

Mini Lessons

Preteaching Vocabulary
____ Context Clues

Grammar
____ Perfect Tenses   ❏ Grammar Transparencies and Copymasters, C116

Viewing and Representing
Art Appreciation
____ *Patrick Henry Before the Virginia House of*
Burgesses by Peter F. Rothermel

Cross Curricular Link

American History
____ Patrick Henry

Informal Assessment
____ Understanding Multiple Word Meanings

Assessment
____ Selection Quiz   ❏ Unit Two Resource Book: Selection Quiz, p. 54
____ Selection Test   ❏ Formal Assessment: Selection Test, pp. 47–48
____ Test Generator

Homework Assignments

_____

_____

_____

_____

_____

Other Teaching Materials

_____

_____

_____

_____

_____

The Declaration of Independence

Core Objectives
- Understand a document of critical importance in U.S. history
- Recognize examples of parallelism
- Construct meaning by paraphrasing difficult passages

MISSOURI PLANNER

Grade-Level Expectations

R1.C, R1.D, R1.E, R1.F, R1.G, R1.H, R1.I, R2.A, R2.C, W1.A

Integrating Skills

Grammar
- Capitalization
- Verbs: Avoiding Shifts

Vocabulary
- Using Context Clues
- Using a Thesaurus

Preparing to Read
____ Connect to Your Life
____ Build Background
____ Vocabulary Preview   ❑ Unit Two Resource Book: Words to Know SkillBuilder, p. 58
____ Focus Your Reading
     Literary Analysis: Parallelism   ❑ Unit Two Resource Book: Literary Analysis SkillBuilder, p. 57
     Active Reading: Paraphrasing   ❑ Unit Two Resource Book: Active Reading SkillBuilder, p. 56

Teaching the Literature
                             ❑ PE pp. 270–281
____ Reading the Selection   ❑ Unit Two Resource Book: Summary, p. 55

Thinking Through the Literature
____ Connect to the Literature
____ Think Critically   ❑ Reading and Critical Thinking Transparencies, T41
____ Extend Interpretations
____ Literary Analysis: Parallelism   ❑ Literary Analysis Transparencies, T10

Choices and Challenges
Writing Options
____ Modern Paraphrase
____ Teenager's Declaration
____ Personal Response

Activities and Explorations
____ Taking Slides
____ First Draft Blues
____ Colonial Cartoon

Vocabulary in Action
____ Context Clues

The Declaration of Independence

Teaching Options (from Teacher's Edition)

Mini Lessons

Preteaching Vocabulary
____ Using Context Clues

Vocabulary Strategy
____ Using a Thesaurus to Determine   ❑ Vocabulary Transparencies and Copymasters, C31
Synonyms

Grammar
____ Capitalization   ❑ Grammar Transparencies and Copymasters, C144
____ Verbs: Avoiding Shifts in Tense, Mood,   ❑ Grammar Transparencies and Copymasters, C120
and Voice

Viewing and Representing
Art Appreciation
____ *Signing the Declaration of Independence*
by John Trumbull

Cross Curricular Links

History
____ The Age of Enlightenment
____ Legal Rights of Women in 1776

Informal Assessment
____ Making Inferences and Drawing Conclusions
____ Retelling

Assessment
____ Selection Quiz   ❑ Unit Two Resource Book: Selection Quiz, p. 59
____ Selection Test   ❑ Formal Assessment: Selection Test, pp. 49–50
____ Test Generator

Homework Assignments

_____

_____

_____

_____

_____

Other Teaching Materials

_____

_____

_____

_____

_____

Name _____ *Date* _____

Letter to the Rev. Samson Occom /
Letter to John Adams

Pages 282–288

Core Objectives
- Understand and appreciate literary letters
- Appreciate author's use of figurative language
- Use strategies for reading literary letters

Integrating Skills

Grammar	Vocabulary
■ Using Correct Verb Forms	■ Using Context Clues

Preparing to Read
____ Connect to Your Life
____ Build Background
____ Vocabulary Preview: Using Context Clues   ❑ Unit Two Resource Book: Words to Know SkillBuilder, p. 64
____ Focus Your Reading
Literary Analysis: Figurative Language   ❑ Unit Two Resource Book: Literary Analysis SkillBuilder, p. 63
Active Reading: Literary Letters   ❑ Unit Two Resource Book: Active Reading SkillBuilder, p. 62

Teaching the Literature
❑ PE pp. 282–288
____ Reading the Selection   ❑ Unit Two Resource Book: Summary, p. 60

Thinking Through the Literature
____ Connect to the Literature
____ Think Critically   ❑ Reading and Critical Thinking Transparencies, T7
____ Extend Interpretations
____ Literary Analysis: Figurative Language

Choices and Challenges
Writing Options
____ Literary Letter

Activities and Explorations
____ Talk Show

Vocabulary in Action
____ Assessment Practice

Letter to the Rev. Samson Occom /
Letter to John Adams

Teaching Options (from Teacher's Edition)

Mini Lessons

Preteaching Vocabulary
____ Using Context Clues

Grammar
____ Using Correct Verb Forms   ❑ Grammar Transparencies and Copymasters, C117

Viewing and Representing
Art Appreciation
____ *The Edenton Ladies Tea Party*

____ ***Informal Assessment***

Assessment

____ Selection Quiz   ❑ Unit Two Resource Book: Selection Quiz, p. 65
____ Selection Test   ❑ Formal Assessment: Selection Test, pp. 51–52
____ Test Generator

Homework Assignments

_____

_____

_____

_____

_____

Other Teaching Materials

_____

_____

_____

_____

_____

What Is an American?

Core Objectives
- Understand and appreciate an essay
- Understand and appreciate use of theme
- Analyze contrast in an essay

> **MISSOURI PLANNER**
> Grade-Level Expectations
> R1.C, R1.D, R1.E, R1.F, R1.G, R1.H, R1.I, R2.A, R2.B, R2.C, W1.A

Integrating Skills

Grammar
- Using Verbs: Voice and Mood

Vocabulary
- Using Context Clues

Preparing to Read
____ Connect to Your Life
____ Build Background
____ Vocabulary Preview: Using Context Clues   ❑ Unit Two Resource Book: Words to Know SkillBuilder, p. 69
____ Focus Your Reading
____ Literary Analysis: Theme   ❑ Unit Two Resource Book: Literary Analysis SkillBuilder, p. 68
____ Active Reading: Analyzing Contrast   ❑ Unit Two Resource Book: Active Reading SkillBuilder, p. 67

Teaching the Literature
                                                      ❑ PE pp. 289–294
____ Reading the Selection   ❑ Unit One Resource Book: Summary, p. 66

Thinking Through the Literature
____ Connect to the Literature
____ Think Critically   ❑ Reading and Critical Thinking Transparencies, T15, T50
____ Extend Interpretations
____ Literary Analysis: Theme   ❑ Literary Analysis Transparencies, T22

Choices and Challenges

Writing Options
____ Draft of Article
____ Local Definition

Vocabulary in Action
____ Context Clues

What Is an American?

Teaching Options (from Teacher's Edition)

Mini Lessons

Preteaching Vocabulary
____ Using Context Clues

Grammar
____ Using Verbs: Voice and Mood ❏ Grammar Transparencies and Copymasters, C119

Viewing and Representing
Art Appreciation
____ *Van Bergen Overmantel*
attributed to John Heaten

Informal Assessment
____ Perceiving Cause and Effect

Assessment

____ Selection Quiz ❏ Unit Two Resource Book: Selection Quiz, p. 70
____ Selection Test ❏ Formal Assessment: Selection Test, p. 53
____ Test Generator

Homework Assignments

_____
_____
_____
_____
_____

Other Teaching Materials

_____
_____
_____
_____
_____

Lecture to a Missionary

Core Objectives
- Understand and appreciate a speech
- Appreciate author's use of tone
- Draw conclusions about tone

```
                    MISSOURI PLANNER
                Grade-Level Expectations
        R1.C, R1.D, R1.F, R1.G, R1.H, R1.I, R2.A, R2.C,
        W1.A
```

Integrating Skills

Grammar
- Commonly Confused Verbs

Vocabulary
- Understanding Figurative Language

Preparing to Read
____ Connect to Your Life
____ Build Background
____ Focus Your Reading
    Literary Analysis: Tone   ❏ Unit Two Resource Book: Literary Analysis SkillBuilder, p. 73
    Active Reading: Drawing Conclusions About Tone   ❏ Unit Two Resource Book: Active Reading SkillBuilder, p. 72

Teaching the Literature
____ Reading the Selection
     ❏ PE pp. 295–299
     ❏ Unit Two Resource Book: Summary, p. 71

Thinking Through the Literature
____ Connect to the Literature
____ Think Critically   ❏ Reading and Critical Thinking Transparencies, T4
____ Extend Interpretations
____ Literary Analysis: Tone   ❏ Literary Analysis Transparencies, T19

Choices and Challenges

Writing Options
____ Mediator's Recommendations
____ Cran's Response
____ Tolerance Pamphlet

Activities and Explorations
____ Re-created Speech
____ Mural of Seneca History

Lecture to a Missionary

Teaching Options (from Teacher's Edition)

Mini Lessons

Vocabulary Strategy
____ Understanding Figurative Language   ❑ Vocabulary Transparencies and Copymasters, C32

Grammar
____ Commonly Confused Verbs   ❑ Grammar Transparencies and Copymasters, C122

Speaking and Listening
____ Speech

Assessment

____ Selection Quiz   ❑ Unit Two Resource Book: Selection Quiz, p. 74
____ Selection Test   ❑ Formal Assessment: Selection Test, p. 55
____ Test Generator

Homework Assignments	Other Teaching Materials

from Stride Toward Freedom /
Necessary to Protect Ourselves

Core Objectives
- Understand and appreciate an excerpt and a transcript of an interview
- Understand the historical context of a literary work
- Analyze the structure of arguments

> **MISSOURI PLANNER**
> Grade-Level Expectations
> R1.C, R1.D, R1.F, R1.G, R1.H, R1.I, R2.A, R2.C, R3.C

Integrating Skills
Grammar
- Past Perfect Tense

Vocabulary
- Using Context Clues
- Connotations and Idioms

Preparing to Read
____ Connect to Your Life
____ Build Background
____ Vocabulary Preview: Using Context Clues   ❏ Unit Two Resource Book: Words to Know SkillBuilder, p. 79
____ Focus Your Reading
     Literary Analysis: Historical Context   ❏ Unit Two Resource Book: Literary Analysis SkillBuilder, p. 78
     Active Reading: Analyzing the Structure   ❏ Unit Two Resource Book: Active Reading SkillBuilder, p. 77
      of Arguments

Teaching the Literature
                                    ❏ PE pp. 300–308
____ Reading the Selection   ❏ Unit Two Resource Book: Summary, p. 76

Thinking Through the Literature
____ Connect to the Literature
____ Think Critically   ❏ Reading and Critical Thinking Transparencies, T17, T21, T23
____ Extend Interpretations
____ Literary Analysis: Historical Context   ❏ Literary Analysis Transparencies, T16

Choices and Challenges
Writing Options
____ Points of Comparison

Vocabulary in Action
____ Word Knowledge

from Stride Toward Freedom /
Necessary to Protect Ourselves

Teaching Options (from Teacher's Edition)

Mini Lessons

Preteaching Vocabulary
____ Using Context Clues

Vocabulary Strategy
____ Understanding Connotations and Idioms ❑ Vocabulary Transparencies and Copymasters, C36

Grammar
____ Past Perfect Tense ❑ Grammar Transparencies and Copymasters, C116

Speaking and Listening
____ Debate

Informal Assessment
____ Identifying the Main Idea

Assessment

____ Selection Quiz ❑ Unit Two Resource Book: Selection Quiz, p. 80
____ Selection Test ❑ Formal Assessment: Selection Test, pp. 57–58
____ Test Generator

Homework Assignments

_____
_____
_____
_____
_____

Other Teaching Materials

_____
_____
_____
_____
_____

I Am Joaquin / Yo Soy Joaquín

Core Objectives
- Understand and appreciate an epic poem
- Use strategies for reading epic poetry

MISSOURI PLANNER
Grade-Level Expectations
R1.C, R1.D, R1.F, R1.G, R1.H, R1.I, R2.A, R2.C, W1.A, W3.C

Integrating Skills

Grammar
- Problems in Using Verb Tenses

Vocabulary
- Researching Word Origins

Preparing to Read
____ Comparing Literature
____ Connect to Your Life
____ Build Background
____ Focus Your Reading
    Literary Analysis: Epic Poem   ❑ Unit Two Resource Book: Literary Analysis SkillBuilder, p. 82
    Active Reading: Strategies for Reading Epic Poetry   ❑ Unit Two Resource Book: Active Reading SkillBuilder, p. 81

Teaching the Literature
____ Reading the Selection   ❑ PE pp. 309–317

Thinking Through the Literature
____ Connect to the Literature
____ Think Critically   ❑ Reading and Critical Thinking Transparencies, T16, T55
____ Extend Interpretations
____ Literary Analysis: Epic Poem   ❑ Literary Analysis Transparencies, T16

Choices and Challenges
Writing Options
____ Book Review
____ Points of Comparison

Activities and Explorations
____ Choral Reading
____ Language Study

Author Activity
____ Rodolfo Gonzales

I Am Joaquin / Yo Soy Joaquín

Teaching Options (from Teacher's Edition)

Mini Lessons

Vocabulary Strategy
____ Researching Word Origins

❏ Vocabulary Transparencies and Copymasters, C43

Speaking and Listening
____ Poetry Reading Workshop

Grammar
____ Problems in Using Verb Tenses

❏ Grammar Transparencies and Copymasters, T46, C121

Viewing and Representing
Art Appreciation
____ *The Farmworkers of Guadalupe*
by Judith F. Baca

Cross Curricular Link

History
____ Cesar Chavez

Informal Assessment

____ Defining Character

Assessment

____ Selection Test

❏ Formal Assessment: Selection Test, pp. 59–60

____ Part Test

❏ Formal Assessment: Unit Two, Part 2, pp. 61–62

____ Test Generator

Homework Assignments

_____

_____

_____

_____

_____

Other Teaching Materials

_____

_____

_____

_____

_____

Persuasive Essay

Writing Prompt

Write a persuasive essay about
an issue that concerns you.

MISSOURI PLANNER
Grade-Level Expectations
R3.D, W1.A, W2.D, W2.E, W2.F, W3.C

Preparing to Read

____ Introduction

____ Basics in a Box

____ Using the Graphic

❑ Writing Transparencies and Copymasters, T11, T20, C27

____ Analyzing a Student Model
"Security Cameras in Schools"

❑ Unit Two Resource Book: Student Models, pp. 89–94

Writing

____ **Prewriting**
Choosing an Issue
Planning Your Persuasive Essay

❑ Unit Two Resource Book: Prewriting, p. 84

____ **Drafting**
Organizing the Draft

❑ Unit Two Resource Book: Drafting and Elaboration, p. 85

____ **Peer Review**
Ask Your Peer Reader

❑ Unit Two Resource Book: Peer Response Guide, pp. 86–87

____ **Revising**
Supporting Personal Opinions with Facts

❑ Unit Two Resource Book: Revising, Editing, and Proofreading, p. 88
❑ Unit Two Resource Book: Rubric for Evaluation, p. 95

____ **Editing and Proofreading**
Pronoun-Antecedent Agreement

____ **Reflecting**

Homework Assignments

_____

_____

_____

_____

_____

Other Teaching Materials

_____

_____

_____

_____

_____

A Psalm of Life

Core Objectives
- Understand and appreciate a classic lyric poem
- Examine stanza and rhyme scheme
- Use strategies for reading traditional poetry

MISSOURI PLANNER
Grade-Level Expectations
R1.C, R1.D, R1.F, R1.G, R1.H, R1.I, R2.A, R2.C, W1.A

Integrating Skills

Grammar	Vocabulary
■ Noun Phrases	■ Homonyms

Preparing to Read
___ Connect to Your Life
___ Build Background
___ Focus Your Reading

Literary Analysis: Stanza and Rhyme Scheme   ❏ Unit Three Resource Book: Literary Analysis SkillBuilder, p. 5

Active Reading: Strategies for   ❏ Unit Three Resource Book: Active Reading SkillBuilder, p. 4
    Reading Traditional Poetry

Teaching the Literature
___ Reading the Selection   ❏ PE pp. 344–348

Thinking Through the Literature
___ Connect to the Literature
___ Think Critically   ❏ Reading and Critical Thinking Transparencies, T51
___ Extend Interpretations
___ Literary Analysis: Stanza and Rhyme Scheme   ❏ Literary Analysis Transparencies, T11

Choices and Challenges
Writing Options
___ Personal Response
___ Longfellow Parody

Activities and Explorations
___ Photo Collage
___ Bumper Sticker

___ **Author Activity**

A Psalm of Life

Teaching Options (from Teacher's Edition)

Mini Lessons

Vocabulary Strategy

___ Homonyms

   ❏ Vocabulary Transparencies and Copymasters, C35

Grammar

___ Noun Phrases

   ❏ Grammar Transparencies and Copymasters, C80

Viewing and Representing

Art Appreciation

___ *En Mer [At Sea]* by Max Bohm

Assessment

___ Selection Test

___ Test Generator

   ❏ Formal Assessment: Selection Test, pp. 63–64

Homework Assignments

_____

_____

_____

_____

_____

Other Teaching Materials

_____

_____

_____

_____

_____

The Devil and Tom Walker

Core Objectives
- Understand and appreciate a short story
- Identify imagery in a short story
- Visualize the characters, setting, and events in a short story

```
┌─────────────────────────────────────────┐
│           MISSOURI PLANNER                │
│        Grade-Level Expectations           │
│ R1.C, R1.D, R1.F, R1.G, R1.H, R1.I, R2.A, R2.C, │
│ W1.A                                      │
└─────────────────────────────────────────┘
```

Integrating Skills

Grammar
- Verbal Phrases: Infinitives, Gerunds, and Participles
- Using Modifiers Correctly

Vocabulary
- Using Context Clues
- Idioms
- Word Origins

Preparing to Read

____ Connect to Your Life

____ Build Background

____ Vocabulary Preview: Using Context Clues   ❑ Unit Three Resource Book: Words to Know SkillBuilder, p. 9

____ Focus Your Reading

      Literary Analysis: Imagery   ❑ Unit Three Resource Book: Literary Analysis SkillBuilder, p. 8

      Active Reading: Visualizing   ❑ Unit Three Resource Book: Active Reading SkillBuilder, p. 7

Teaching the Literature

      ❑ PE pp. 349–362

____ Reading the Selection   ❑ Unit Three Resource Book: Summary, p. 6

Thinking Through the Literature

____ Connect to the Literature

____ Think Critically   ❑ Reading and Critical Thinking Transparencies, T8

____ Extend Interpretations

____ Literary Analysis: Imagery   ❑ Literary Analysis Transparencies, T18, T24

Choices and Challenges

Writing Options

____ Reflective Essay on Wealth

____ Fitting Proverbs

____ Updated Faust Legend

Activities and Explorations

____ Board Game

Vocabulary in Action

____ Assessment Practice

____ Meaning Clues

Author Activity

____ Tales Compared

The Devil and Tom Walker

Teaching Options (from Teacher's Edition)

Mini Lessons

Preteaching Vocabulary
____ Using Context Clues

Vocabulary Strategy
____ Idioms   ❏ Vocabulary Transparencies and Copymasters, C36
____ Word Origins

Grammar
____ Verbal Phrases: Infinitives, Gerunds,
and Participles
____ Using Modifiers Correctly   ❏ Grammar Transparencies and Copymasters, C127

Cross Curricular Links

Multicultural
____ Folklore

Economics
____ Usury

Informal Assessment
____ Story Map
____ Recognize Facts and Details

Assessment
____ Selection Quiz   ❏ Unit Three Resource Book: Selection Quiz, p. 10
____ Selection Test   ❏ Formal Assessment: Selection Test, pp. 65–66
____ Test Generator

Homework Assignments

_____

_____

_____

_____

_____

Other Teaching Materials

_____

_____

_____

_____

_____

Name _____ *Date* _____

from Self-Reliance

Pages 363–368

Core Objectives
- Understand and appreciate a transcendentalist essay
- Appreciate author's use of aphorisms
- Use summarizing to understand an essay

<table>
<tr><td colspan="2">MISSOURI PLANNER</td></tr>
<tr><td colspan="2">Grade-Level Expectations</td></tr>
<tr><td colspan="2">R1.C, R1.D, R1.E, R1.F, R1.G, R1.H, R1.I, R2.A, R2.C, W1.A, W3.C, IL1.A, IL1.B, IL1.C</td></tr>
</table>

Integrating Skills

Grammar
- Adjective and Adverb Phrases

Vocabulary
- Context Clues

Preparing to Read
____ Connect to Your Life
____ Build Background
____ Vocabulary Preview: Using Context Clues   ❑ Unit Three Resource Book: Words to Know SkillBuilder, p. 14
____ Focus Your Reading
     Literary Analysis: Aphorism   ❑ Unit Three Resource Book: Literary Analysis SkillBuilder, p. 13
     Active Reading: Summarizing   ❑ Unit Three Resource Book: Active Reading SkillBuilder, p. 12

Teaching the Literature
  ❑ PE pp. 363–368
____ Reading the Selection   ❑ Unit Three Resource Book: Summary, p. 11

Thinking Through the Literature
____ Connect to the Literature
____ Think Critically   ❑ Reading and Critical Thinking Transparencies, T10
____ Extend Interpretations
____ Literary Analysis: Aphorism   ❑ Literary Analysis Transparencies, T8

Choices and Challenges
Writing Options
____ Personal Essay
____ Update of Emerson

Inquiry and Research
____ History

Vocabulary in Action
____ Meaning Clues

____ **Author Activity**

from Self-Reliance

Teaching Options (from Teacher's Edition)

Mini Lessons

Preteaching Vocabulary
____ Using Context Clues

Grammar   ❏ Grammar Transparencies and Copymasters, C82
____ Modifiers: Adjective and Adverb
Phrases

Viewing and Representing
Art Appreciation
____ *Kindred Spirits* by Asher B. Durand

Informal Assessment
____ Recognize the Author's Point of View
and Purpose

Assessment
____ Selection Quiz   ❏ Unit Three Resource Book: Selection Quiz, p. 15
____ Selection Test   ❏ Formal Assessment: Selection Test, pp. 67–68
____ Test Generator

Homework Assignments

_____

_____

_____

_____

_____

Other Teaching Materials

_____

_____

_____

_____

_____

from Civil Disobedience

Core Objectives
- Understand and appreciate a persuasive essay
- Use strategies for reading essays

Integrating Skills

MISSOURI PLANNER
Grade-Level Expectations
R1.C, R1.D, R1.E, R1.F, R1.G, R1.H, R1.I, R2.A, R2.C, W1.A, W3.C, IL1.A, IL1.B, IL1.C

Grammar
- Adjective and Adverb Phrases
- Compound Adjectives

Vocabulary
- Using Context Clues
- Connotation and Denotation

Preparing to Read
____ Connect to Your Life
____ Build Background
____ Vocabulary Preview: Using Context Clues   ❑ Unit Three Resource Book: Words to Know SkillBuilder, p. 19
____ Focus Your Reading
     Literary Analysis: Essay   ❑ Unit Three Resource Book: Literary Analysis SkillBuilder, p. 18
     Active Reading: Strategies for Reading Essays   ❑ Unit Three Resource Book: Active Reading SkillBuilder, p. 17

Teaching the Literature
                             ❑ PE pp. 369–380
____ Reading the Selection   ❑ Unit Three Resource Book: Summary, p. 16

Thinking Through the Literature
____ Connect to the Literature
____ Think Critically   ❑ Reading and Critical Thinking Transparencies, T15, T20
____ Extend Interpretations
____ Literary Analysis: Essay   ❑ Literary Analysis Transparencies, T8, T9

Choices and Challenges

Writing Options
____ Comparison of Emerson and Thoreau
____ Personal Response
____ Essay on Citizenship

Activities and Explorations
____ Group Discussion
____ Drama in a Jailhouse
____ Political Poster

Inquiry and Research
____ Resisting Injustice

Vocabulary in Action
____ Context Clues

from Civil Disobedience

Teaching Options (from Teacher's Edition)

Mini Lessons

Preteaching Vocabulary
____ Using Context Clues

Vocabulary Strategy
____ Understanding Connotative and
Denotative Meanings of Words

❑ Vocabulary Transparencies and Copymasters, C38

Grammar
____ Modifiers: Adjective and
Adverb Phrases
____ Compound Adjectives

Viewing and Representing
Art Appreciation
____ Photographs

Inquiry and Research
____ Generating Relevant Questions

Cross Curricular Links

History
____ U.S.-Mexican War

Social Studies
____ Female Leaders of Social Protest

Informal Assessment
____ Idea Chart

Assessment
____ Selection Quiz
____ Selection Test
____ Test Generator

❑ Unit Three Resource Book: Selection Quiz, p. 20
❑ Formal Assessment: Selection Test, pp. 69–70

Homework Assignments

_____
_____
_____
_____
_____

Other Teaching Materials

_____
_____
_____
_____
_____

from Walden

Core Objectives
- Understand and appreciate a classic example of nature writing
- Evaluate the author's observations in an essay

Integrating Skills

Grammar	Vocabulary
• Modifiers: *Good* and *Well*	• Using Context Clues
	• Homonyms
• Modifiers: Nouns as Adjectives	
• Double Negatives	

> **MISSOURI PLANNER**
> Grade-Level Expectations
> R1.C, R1.D, R1.F, R1.G, R1.H, R1.I, R2.A, R2.B, R2.C, R3.B W1.A, IL1.A, IL1.B, IL1.C

Preparing to Read
____ Connect to Your Life
____ Build Background
____ Vocabulary Preview: Using Context Clues   ❏ Unit Three Resource Book: Words to Know SkillBuilder, p. 24
____ Focus Your Reading
      Literary Analysis: Nature Writing   ❏ Unit Three Resource Book: Literary Analysis SkillBuilder, p. 23
      Active Reading: Evaluating Author's   ❏ Unit Three Resource Book: Active Reading SkillBuilder, p. 22
      Observations

Teaching the Literature
                                             ❏ PE pp. 381–393
____ Reading the Selection   ❏ Unit Three Resource Book: Summary, p. 21

Thinking Through the Literature
____ Connect to the Literature
____ Think Critically   ❏ Reading and Critical Thinking Transparencies, T46
____ Extend Interpretations
____ Literary Analysis: Nature Writing   ❏ Literary Analysis Transparencies, T8, T22

Choices and Challenges
Writing Options
____ Letter from Walden Pond
____ Interpretive Essay
____ Nature Writing

Activities and Explorations
____ Photo Essay

Inquiry and Research
____ Walden Today

Vocabulary in Action
____ Assessment Practice
____ Idioms

Teaching Options (from Teacher's Edition)

Mini Lessons

Preteaching Vocabulary
____ Using Context Clues

Vocabulary Strategy
____ Homonyms   ❏ Vocabulary Transparencies and Copymasters, C35

Grammar
____ Modifiers: *Good* and *Well*
____ Modifiers: Nouns as Adjectives
____ Double Negatives

Viewing and Representing
Art Appreciation
____ Photo by Ernst Haas

Cross Curricular Links

Workplace
____ Setting Goals

Social Studies
____ Nature Conservation

Informal Assessment
____ Make Inferences and Draw Conclusions
____ Journal Entry

Assessment
____ Selection Quiz   ❏ Unit Three Resource Book: Selection Quiz, p. 25
____ Selection Test   ❏ Formal Assessment: Selection Test, pp. 71–72
____ Test Generator

Homework Assignments

_____
_____
_____
_____
_____

Other Teaching Materials

_____
_____
_____
_____
_____

Selected Poems by Walt Whitman

Core Objectives
- Understand and appreciate three classic poems
- Identify and understand free verse and Whitman's poetic devices for creating rhythm
- Apply strategies for reading free verse

MISSOURI PLANNER
Grade-Level Expectations
R1.C, R1.D, R1.F, R1.G, R1.H, R1.I, R2.A, R2.C

Integrating Skills
Grammar
- Prepositional Phrases
- Placement of Prepositional Phrases

Vocabulary
- Understanding Analogies

Preparing to Read
____ Connect to Your Life
____ Build Background
____ Focus Your Reading
　　 Literary Analysis: Free Verse ❑ Unit Three Resource Book: Literary Analysis SkillBuilder, p. 27
　　 Active Reading: Strategies for Reading ❑ Unit Three Resource Book: Active Reading SkillBuilder, p. 26
　　　 Free Verse

Teaching the Literature
____ Reading the Selection ❑ PE pp. 396–405

Thinking Through the Literature
____ Connect to the Literature
____ Think Critically ❑ Reading and Critical Thinking Transparencies, T15
____ Extend Interpretations
____ Literary Analysis: Free Verse ❑ Literary Analysis Transparencies, T12

Choices and Challenges
Writing Options
____ Literary Review
____ Free Verse Poem

Activities and Explorations
____ Collage of Images
____ Interpretive Dance

Author Activity
____ Neruda's Whitman

Selected Poems by Walt Whitman

Teaching Options (from Teacher's Edition)

Mini Lessons

Vocabulary Strategy
____ Understanding Analogies   ❏ Vocabulary Transparencies and Copymasters, C48

Grammar
____ Prepositional Phrases   ❏ Grammar Transparencies and Copymasters, T11, C83, C84
____ Placement of Prepositional Phrases

Speaking and Listening
____ Choral Reading

Viewing and Representing
Art Appreciation
____ *Cliff Dwellers* by George Bellows

Cross Curricular Link

History
____ Urban and Rural Life—1800s and Today

Assessment

____ Selection Test   ❏ Formal Assessment: Selection Test, pp. 73–74
____ Test Generator

Homework Assignments

_____
_____
_____
_____
_____

Other Teaching Materials

_____
_____
_____
_____
_____

Danse Russe / anyone lived in a pretty how town   Pages 410–415

Core Objectives
- Understand and appreciate experimental poetry
- Make inferences to understand poetry

MISSOURI PLANNER
Grade-Level Expectations
R1.C, R1.D, R1.F, R1.G, R1.H, R1.I, R2.A, R2.C,
W1.A, W3.C, IL.2.A

Preparing to Read
____ Comparing Literature
____ Build Background
____ Focus Your Reading
     Literary Analysis: Experimental Poetry   ❏ Unit Three Resource Book: Literary Analysis SkillBuilder, p. 29
     Active Reading: Making Inferences   ❏ Unit Three Resource Book: Active Reading SkillBuilder, p. 28

Teaching the Literature
____ Reading the Selection   ❏ PE pp. 410–415

Thinking Through the Literature
____ Connect to the Literature
____ Think Critically   ❏ Reading and Critical Thinking Transparencies, T7
____ Extend Interpretations
____ Literary Analysis: Experimental Poetry   ❏ Literary Analysis Transparencies, T12

Choices and Challenges
Writing Options
____ Diary Confession
____ Headstone Inscription
____ Points of Comparison

Activities and Explorations
____ Animation, Anyone?

Author Activity
____ Williams on Video
____ Cummings's Voice

Danse Russe / anyone lived in a pretty how town

Teaching Options (from Teacher's Edition)

Mini Lessons

Speaking and Listening
___ Interpreting Poems

Viewing and Representing
Art Appreciation
___ *Icarus* by Henri Matisse

Informal Assessment
___ Identifying and Comparing Themes

Assessment

___ Selection Test

___ Test Generator

❑ Formal Assessment: Selection Test, pp. 75–76

Homework Assignments

_____

_____

_____

_____

_____

Other Teaching Materials

_____

_____

_____

_____

_____

Ending Poem / Tia Chucha

Core Objectives
■ Understand and appreciate poetry that explores
  cultural and individual identity
■ Identify and understand the speaker of a poem
■ Understand structure and form in poetry

```
┌─────────────────────────────────────┐
│           MISSOURI PLANNER           │
│        Grade-Level Expectations      │
│  R1.C, R1.D, R1.F, R1.G, R1.H, R1.I, R2.A, R2.C, │
│  W1.A, W3.C, IL1.A, IL1.B, IL1.C     │
└─────────────────────────────────────┘
```

Integrating Skills
Vocabulary
■ Using Reference Materials

Preparing to Read
____ Comparing Literature
____ Build Background
____ Focus Your Reading
    Literary Analysis: Speaker   ❑ Unit Three Resource Book: Literary Analysis SkillBuilder, p. 31
    Active Reading: Structure and Form in Poetry   ❑ Unit Three Resource Book: Active Reading SkillBuilder, p. 30

Teaching the Literature
____ Reading the Selection   ❑ PE pp. 416–423

Thinking Through the Literature
____ Connect to the Literature
____ Think Critically   ❑ Reading and Critical Thinking Transparencies, T15
____ Extend Interpretations
____ Literary Analysis: Speaker   ❑ Literary Analysis Transparencies, T11, T20

Choices and Challenges
Writing Options
____ Points of Comparison
____ Autobiographical Sketch or Poem
____ Contrast Essay

Activities and Explorations
____ Paired Reading
____ Monologue
____ Self-Representation

____ **Art Connection**

Inquiry and Research
____ Puerto Rican History

Teaching Options (from Teacher's Edition)

Mini Lessons

Vocabulary Strategy
____ Using Reference Materials   ❏ Vocabulary Transparencies and Copymasters: C40

Speaking and Listening
____ Pronouncing Spanish Words

Viewing and Representing
Art Appreciation
____ *In My Grandmother's Garden*
by Rosario Morales

Cross Curricular Link

History
____ The Chicano Movement

Informal Assessment
____ Figurative Language

Assessment
____ Selection Test   ❏ Formal Assessment: Selection Test: pp. 77–78
____ Test Generator

Homework Assignments
_____
_____
_____
_____
_____

Other Teaching Materials
_____
_____
_____
_____
_____

Gary Keillor

Core Objectives
- Understand and appreciate an autobiographical story
- Identify examples of humor in the story
- Consider the purpose for reading the story

```
┌─────────────────────────────────────────┐
│            MISSOURI PLANNER               │
│        Grade-Level Expectations           │
│ R1.C, R1.D, R1.F, R1.G, R1.H, R1.I, R2.A, R2.C, │
│ W1.A                                      │
└─────────────────────────────────────────┘
```

Integrating Skills

Grammar
- Appositives and Appositive Phrases
- Commas and Parenthetical Expressions

Vocabulary
- Using Context to Determine Meaning of Idioms

Preparing to Read
____ Comparing Literature
____ Build Background
____ Focus Your Reading
     Literary Analysis: Humor   ❏ Unit Three Resource Book: Literary Analysis SkillBuilder, p. 34
     Active Reading: Purpose For Reading   ❏ Unit Three Resource Book: Active Reading SkillBuilder, p. 33

Teaching the Literature
     ❏ PE pp. 424–435
____ Reading the Selection   ❏ Unit Three Resource Book: Summary, p. 32

Thinking Through the Literature
____ Connect to the Literature
____ Think Critically   ❏ Reading and Critical Thinking Transparencies, T23
____ Extend Interpretations
____ Literary Analysis: Humor

Choices and Challenges
Writing Options
____ Points of Comparison
____ Story Sequel
____ Literary Review

Activities and Explorations
____ Drawn-Out Story
____ Comic Recitation

____ **Art Connection**

Author Activity
____ Good Humor

Gary Keillor

Teaching Options (from Teacher's Edition)

Mini Lessons

Vocabulary Strategy
____ Using Context to Determine Meaning of Idioms

❑ Vocabulary Transparencies and Copymasters, C41

Grammar
____ Appositives and Appositive Phrases

❑ Grammar Transparencies and Copymasters, C85

____ Commas with Parenthetical Expressions

❑ Grammar Transparencies and Copymasters, C148

Speaking and Listening
____ Radio Performance

Viewing and Representing
Art Appreciation
____ *Play Within a Play* by David Hockney

Cross Curricular Link

Social Studies
____ Oral Storytelling

Informal Assessment
____ Journal Entries

Assessment
____ Selection Quiz

❑ Unit Three Resource Book: Selection Quiz, p. 35

____ Selection Test

❑ Formal Assessment: Selection Test, pp. 79-80

____ Part Test

❑ Formal Assessment: Unit Three, Part 1 Test, pp. 81–82

____ Test Generator

Homework Assignments

_____
_____
_____
_____
_____

Other Teaching Materials

_____
_____
_____
_____
_____

Reflective Essay

Writing Prompt

Write an essay in which you reflect on an
experience that taught you an important lesson.

> **MISSOURI PLANNER**
> Grade-Level Expectations
> R3.D, W1.A, W2.B, W2.D, W2.E, W3.C

Preparing to Read

____ Introduction

____ Basics in a Box

____ Using the Graphic

❑ Writing Transparencies and Copymasters, T11, T20, C28

____ Analyzing a Student Model
"Eternally Slow"

❑ Unit Three Resource Book: Student Models, pp. 42–47

Writing

____ **Prewriting**
Choosing a Subject
Planning the Reflective Essay

❑ Unit Three Resource Book: Prewriting, p. 37

____ **Drafting**
Organizing the Draft

❑ Unit Three Resource Book: Drafting and Elaboration, p. 38

____ **Peer Review**
Ask Your Peer Reader

❑ Unit Three Resource Book: Peer Response Guide, pp. 39–40

____ **Revising**
Avoiding Clichés

❑ Unit Three Resource Book: Revising, Editing, and Proofreading, p. 41
❑ Unit Three Resource Book: Rubric for Evaluation, p. 48

____ **Editing and Proofreading**
Possessives and Plurals

____ **Reflecting**

Homework Assignments

_____
_____
_____
_____
_____

Other Teaching Materials

_____
_____
_____
_____
_____

The Masque of the Red Death

Core Objectives
- Understand and appreciate a classic short story
- Recognize and interpret allegory
- Clarify meaning in a short story

MISSOURI PLANNER

Grade-Level Expectations

R1.C, R1.D, R1.F, R1.G, R1.H, R1.I, R2.A, R2.C, W1.A, IL1.A, IL1.B, IL1.C

Integrating Skills

Grammar
- Participles and Participial Phrases
- Past and Present Participles

Vocabulary
- Context Clues
- Latin Root Words

Preparing to Read
____ Connect to Your Life
____ Build Background
____ Vocabulary Preview: Using Context Clues   ❏ Unit Three Resource Book: Words to Know SkillBuilder, p. 54
____ Focus Your Reading
____ Literary Analysis: Allegory   ❏ Unit Three Resource Book: Literary Analysis SkillBuilder, p. 53
____ Active Reading: Clarifying Meaning   ❏ Unit Three Resource Book: Active Reading SkillBuilder, p. 52

Teaching the Literature
____ Reading the Selection   ❏ PE pp. 454–463

Thinking Through the Literature
____ Connect to the Literature
____ Think Critically   ❏ Reading and Critical Thinking Transparencies, T10
____ Extend Interpretations
____ Literary Analysis: Allegory

Choices and Challenges

Writing Options
____ Newspaper Editorial
____ Poetic Retelling
____ Archaeological Report

Activities and Explorations
____ A Fantastic Set
____ Radio Drama

Inquiry and Research
____ Medical Detective

Vocabulary in Action
____ Word Knowledge

The Masque of the Red Death

Teaching Options (from Teacher's Edition)

Mini Lessons

Preteaching Vocabulary
____ Using Context Clues

Vocabulary Strategy
____ Applying Meanings of Latin Root Words   ❏ Vocabulary Transparencies and Copymasters, C42

Grammar
____ Participles and Participial Phrases   ❏ Grammar Transparencies and Copymasters, C86
____ Using Past and Present Participles   ❏ Grammar Transparencies and Copymasters, C87

Speaking and Listening
____ Nonverbal Communication

Viewing and Representing
Art Appreciation
____ *Il ridotto [The Foyer]* by Pietro Longhi

Informal Assessment
____ Storyboard

Assessment
____ Selection Quiz   ❏ Unit Three Resource Book: Selection Quiz, p. 55
____ Selection Test   ❏ Formal Assessment: Selection Test, pp. 83–84
____ Test Generator

Homework Assignments

_____

_____

_____

_____

_____

Other Teaching Materials

_____

_____

_____

_____

_____

The Raven

Core Objectives
- Understand and appreciate a classic narrative poem
- Identify and analyze sound devices in a poem
- Draw conclusions about the speaker in a poem

```
┌──────────────────────────────────────┐
│           MISSOURI PLANNER            │
│       Grade-Level Expectations        │
│ R1.C, R1.D, R1.F, R1.G, R1.H, R1.I, R2.A, R2.C, │
│ W1.A, IL1.A, IL1.B, IL1.C             │
└──────────────────────────────────────┘
```

Integrating Skills

Grammar
- Comparative Forms of Adjectives and Adverbs

Vocabulary
- Using Context Clues

Preparing to Read
____ Connect to Your Life
____ Build Background
____ Vocabulary Preview: Using Context Clues   ❏ Unit Three Resource Book: Words to Know SkillBuilder, p. 59
____ Focus Your Reading
     Literary Analysis: Sound Devices   ❏ Unit Three Resource Book: Literary Analysis SkillBuilder, p. 58
     Active Reading: Drawing Conclusions   ❏ Unit Three Resource Book: Active Reading SkillBuilder, p. 57

Teaching the Literature
                                           ❏ PE pp. 466–472
____ Reading the Selection   ❏ Unit Three Resource Book: Summary, p. 56

Thinking Through the Literature
____ Connect to the Literature
____ Think Critically   ❏ Reading and Critical Thinking Transparencies, T4
____ Extend Interpretations
____ Literary Analysis: Sound Devices   ❏ Literary Analysis Transparencies, T12

Choices and Challenges

Writing Options
____ Prose Description
____ Speaker's Diary Entry
____ Poetic Parody

Activities and Explorations
____ Dramatic Reading
____ Image of the Study

Inquiry and Research
____ Psychological View

Vocabulary in Action
____ Meaning Clues

The Raven

Teaching Options (from Teacher's Edition)

Mini Lessons

Preteaching Vocabulary
____ Using Context Clues

Grammar
____ Comparative Forms of Adjectives and   ❏ Grammar Transparencies and Copymasters, C128
Adverbs

Speaking and Listening
____ Dramatic Reading

Informal Assessment
____ Evaluating the Speaker

Assessment

____ Selection Quiz   ❏ Unit Three Resource Book: Selection Quiz, p. 60
____ Selection Test   ❏ Formal Assessment: Selection Test, pp. 85–86
____ Test Generator

Homework Assignments	**Other Teaching Materials**
_____	_____
_____	_____
_____	_____
_____	_____
_____	

The Fall of the House of Usher

Core Objectives
- Understand and appreciate a classic Gothic short story
- Identify and understand mood in a short story
- Understand complex sentences

MISSOURI PLANNER

Grade-Level Expectations

R1.C, R1.D, R1.E, R1.F, R1.G, R1.H, R1.I, R2.A, R2.B, R2.C, W1.A, IL1.A, IL1.B, IL1.C

Integrating Skills

Grammar
- Irregular Adjectives and Adverbs
- Apostrophes: Possessive Compounds
- Dashes

Vocabulary
- Context Clues
- Understanding Prefixes
- Understanding Figurative Language

Preparing to Read
____ Connect to Your Life
____ Build Background
____ Vocabulary Preview: Using Context Clues   ❏ Unit Three Resource Book: Words to Know SkillBuilder, p. 64
____ Focus Your Reading
     Literary Analysis: Mood   ❏ Unit Three Resource Book: Literary Analysis SkillBuilder, p. 63
     Active Reading: Understanding Complex   ❏ Unit Three Resource Book: Active Reading SkillBuilder, p. 62
     Sentences

Teaching the Literature   ❏ PE pp. 473–499
____ Reading the Selection   ❏ Unit Three Resource Book: Summary, p. 61

Thinking Through the Literature
____ Connect to the Literature
____ Think Critically   ❏ Reading and Critical Thinking Transparencies, T12, T15, T49
____ Extend Interpretations
____ Literary Analysis: Mood   ❏ Literary Analysis Transparencies, T18

Choices and Challenges
Writing Options
____ Roderick Usher's Letter
____ Comparing Ushers
____ Madeline's Retelling

Activities and Explorations
____ Eerie Pantomime
____ Usher Poster
____ Charting Usher Events

Inquiry and Research
____ Science

Vocabulary in Action
____ Context Clues/Meaning Clues

The Fall of the House of Usher

Teaching Options (from Teacher's Edition)

Mini Lessons

Preteaching Vocabulary
____ Using Context Clues

Vocabulary Strategy
____ Understanding Prefixes   ❏ Vocabulary Transparencies and Copymasters, C44
____ Understanding Figurative Language

Grammar
____ Comparisons of Irregular Adjectives and   ❏ Grammar Transparencies and Copymasters, T52, C129
Adverbs
____ Apostrophes: Possessive Compounds   ❏ Grammar Transparencies and Copymasters, C160
____ Dashes   ❏ Grammar Transparencies and Copymasters, C161

Speaking and Listening
____ Oral Reading
____ Dramatic Reading

Viewing and Representing
Art Appreciation
____ *Self Portrait* by Bertalan Szekely
____ *Head of Ophelia* by Edwin Austin Abbey

Cross Curricular Links

Humanities
____ Gothic Architecture

Psychology
____ Twins

Informal Assessment
____ Describing Plot, Setting, Character, and Mood
____ Journal Entry

Assessment
____ Selection Quiz   ❏ Unit Three Resource Book: Selection Quiz, p. 65
____ Selection Test   ❏ Formal Assessment: Selection Test, pp. 87–88
____ Test Generator

Homework Assignments

_____

_____

_____

_____

Other Teaching Materials

_____

_____

_____

_____

Dr. Heidegger's Experiment

Core Objectives
- Understand and appreciate a classic short story that explores a Gothic theme
- Identify and understand foreshadowing
- Interpret the story as an allegory

MISSOURI PLANNER
Grade-Level Expectations
R1.C, R1.D, R1.F, R1.G, R1.H, R1.I, R2.A, R2.C, W1.A

Integrating Skills

Grammar
- Comparatives
- Avoiding Illogical Comparisons

Vocabulary
- Using Context Clues
- Applying Meaning of Suffixes

Preparing to Read
____ Connect to Your Life
____ Build Background
____ Vocabulary Preview: Using Context Clues   ❑ Unit Three Resource Book: Words to Know SkillBuilder, p. 69
____ Focus Your Reading
       Literary Analysis: Foreshadowing   ❑ Unit Three Resource Book: Literary Analysis SkillBuilder, p. 68
       Active Reading: Interpreting Allegory   ❑ Unit Three Resource Book: Active Reading SkillBuilder, p. 67

Teaching the Literature
                                                    ❑ PE pp. 500–515
____ Reading the Selection   ❑ Unit Three Resource Book: Summary, p. 66

Thinking Through the Literature
____ Connect to the Literature
____ Think Critically   ❑ Reading and Critical Thinking Transparencies, T2, T15
____ Extend Interpretations
____ Literary Analysis: Foreshadowing

Choices and Challenges
Writing Options
____ Warning Label
____ Science News
____ Story Ending

Activities and Explorations
____ Product Chart

Vocabulary in Action
____ Assessment Practice

Dr. Heidegger's Experiment

Teaching Options (from Teacher's Edition)

Mini Lessons

Preteaching Vocabulary
____ Using Context Clues

Vocabulary Strategy
____ Applying Meanings of Suffixes   ❏ Vocabulary Transparencies and Copymasters, C46

Grammar
____ Comparatives
____ Avoiding Illogical Comparisons

Speaking and Listening
____ Interpreting Character

Viewing and Representing
Art Appreciation
____ *Déjeuner [Luncheon]* by Gustave Caillebotte
____ *La Danse à la Campagne [The country dance]* by Pierre Auguste Renoir

Cross Curricular Links

History
____ Ponce de Leon and the Fountain of Youth

Multicultural
____ Attitudes Toward Aging

Informal Assessment
____ Changing Point of View
____ Choosing the Best Summary

Assessment
____ Selection Quiz   ❏ Unit Three Resource Book: Selection Quiz, p. 70
____ Selection Test   ❏ Formal Assessment: Selection Test, pp. 89–90
____ Test Generator

Homework Assignments
_____
_____
_____
_____
_____

Other Teaching Materials
_____
_____
_____
_____
_____

A Rose for Emily

Core Objectives
- Understand and appreciate a short story
- Identify and understand characterization
- Understand the sequence of events in the story

MISSOURI PLANNER

Grade-Level Expectations

R1.C, R1.D, R1.E, R1.F, R1.G, R1.H, R1.I, R2.A, R2.C, W1.A, IL1.A, IL1.B, IL1.C, IL.2.A

Integrating Skills

Grammar
- Superlatives
- Modifiers:
  Illogical Comparisons

Vocabulary
- Using Context Clues
- Connotation

Preparing to Read
____ Comparing Literature
____ Build Background
____ Vocabulary Preview: Using Context Clues   ❑ Unit Three Resource Book: Words to Know SkillBuilder, p. 74
____ Focus Your Reading
     Literary Analysis: Characterization   ❑ Unit Three Resource Book: Literary Analysis SkillBuilder, p. 73
     Active Reading: Sequencing Events   ❑ Unit Three Resource Book: Active Reading SkillBuilder, p. 72

Teaching the Literature
                                            ❑ PE pp. 516–527
____ Reading the Selection   ❑ Unit Three Resource Book: Summary, p. 71

Thinking Through the Literature
____ Connect to the Literature
____ Think Critically   ❑ Reading and Critical Thinking Transparencies, T13, T15
____ Extend Interpretations
____ Literary Analysis: Foreshadowing   ❑ Literary Analysis Transparencies, T6

Choices and Challenges

Writing Options
____ Obituary for Miss Emily
____ Secret Diary
____ Points of Comparison

Activities and Explorations
____ Short Story Video
____ Theatrical Performance

Inquiry and Research
____ The New South

Vocabulary in Action
____ Context Clues

A Rose for Emily

Teaching Options (from Teacher's Edition)

Mini Lessons

Preteaching Vocabulary
____ Using Context Clues

Vocabulary Strategy
____ Connotation ❑ Vocabulary Transparencies and Copymasters, C47

Grammar
____ Superlatives
____ Modifiers: Illogical Comparisons

Speaking and Listening
____ Dramatic Performance

Viewing and Representing
Art Appreciation
____ *German Teapot* by Charles Warren Mundy
____ *Woman in Distress* by James Ensor

Cross Curricular Link

Workplace
____ Writing Instructions/Problem Solving

Informal Assessment
____ News Report

Assessment
____ Selection Quiz   ❑ Unit Three Resource Book: Selection Quiz, p. 75
____ Selection Test   ❑ Formal Assessment: Selection Test, pp. 91–92
____ Test Generator

Homework Assignments

_____
_____
_____
_____
_____

Other Teaching Materials

_____
_____
_____
_____
_____

Selection Lesson Plan   *Name* _____   *Date* _____

The Life You Save May Be Your Own   **Pages 528–541**

....

Core Objectives
- Understand and appreciate a Southern Gothic short story
- Identify and examine irony
- Draw conclusions about characters

┌───┐
│   **MISSOURI PLANNER**   │
│   Grade-Level Expectations   │
│ R1.C, R1.D, R1.F, R1.G, R1.H, R1.I, R2.A, R2.C, │
│ W1.A, W3.C, IL1.A, IL1.B, IL1.C   │
└───┘

Integrating Skills

Grammar   **Vocabulary**
- Modifiers: - Using Context Clues
  Double Negatives   - Analogies

Preparing to Read
____ Comparing Literature
____ Build Background
____ Vocabulary Preview: Using Context Clues   ❏ Unit Three Resource Book: Words to Know SkillBuilder, p. 79
____ Focus Your Reading
    Literary Analysis: Irony   ❏ Unit Three Resource Book: Literary Analysis SkillBuilder, p. 78
    Active Reading: Drawing Conclusions   ❏ Unit Three Resource Book: Active Reading SkillBuilder, p. 77
      About Characters

Teaching the Literature
____ Reading the Selection   ❏ PE pp. 528–541
____ Reading the Selection   ❏ Unit Three Resource Book: Summary, p. 76

Thinking Through the Literature
____ Connect to the Literature
____ Think Critically   ❏ Reading and Critical Thinking Transparencies, T4
____ Extend Interpretations
____ Literary Analysis: Irony   ❏ Literary Analysis Transparencies, T21

Choices and Challenges
Writing Options
____ Letter of Opinion
____ Sequel: The Saga Continues
____ Points of Comparison

Activities and Explorations
____ Wanted Poster
____ Points of Comparison

Inquiry and Research
____ Con Artists
____ Antisocial Personalities

Vocabulary in Action
____ Assessment Practice

Author Activity
____ The Writer's Eye

The Language of Literature, Grade 11   **85**

The Life You Save May Be Your Own

Teaching Options (from Teacher's Edition)

Mini Lessons

Preteaching Vocabulary
____ Using Context Clues

Vocabulary Strategy
____ Analogies   ❑ Vocabulary Transparencies and Copymasters, C48

Grammar
____ Modifiers: Double Negatives   ❑ Grammar Transparencies and Copymasters, T53, C137

Speaking and Listening
____ Dramatic Presentation

Viewing and Representing
Art Appreciation
____ *Mrs. Gamely* by George Luks
____ *The Interloper* by Billy Morrow Jackson
____ *Road to Rhome* by Alexander Hogue

Cross Curricular Link

History
____ Henry Ford

Informal Assessment

____ Making Inferences
____ Storyboard

Assessment

____ Selection Quiz   ❑ Unit Three Resource Book: Selection Quiz, p. 80
____ Selection Test   ❑ Formal Assessment: Selection Test, pp. 93–94
____ Part Test   ❑ Formal Assessment: Unit Three, Part 2 Test, pp. 95–96
____ Test Generator

Homework Assignments

_____

_____

_____

_____

_____

Other Teaching Materials

_____

_____

_____

_____

_____

Short Story

Writing Prompt
Write a short story. You might choose
to use a surprise ending or twist.

MISSOURI PLANNER
Grade-Level Expectations
R3.D, W1.A, W2.D, W2.E, W2.F

Preparing to Read

____ Introduction

____ Basics in a Box

____ Using the Graphic

❑ Writing Transparencies and Copymasters, T11, T20, C29

____ Analyzing a Student Model
"Reunited"

❑ Unit Three Resource Book: Student Models, pp. 87–92

Writing

____ **Prewriting**
Choosing a Story Idea
Planning the Short Story

❑ Unit Three Resource Book: Prewriting, p. 82

____ **Drafting**
Organizing the Draft

❑ Unit Three Resource Book: Drafting and Elaboration, p. 83

____ **Peer Review**
Ask Your Peer Reader

❑ Unit Three Resource Book: Peer Response Guide, pp. 84–85

____ **Revising**
Using Dialogue

❑ Unit Three Resource Book: Revising, Editing, and Proofreading, p. 86
❑ Unit Three Resource Book: Rubric for Evaluation, p. 93

____ **Editing and Proofreading**
Punctuating Dialogue

____ **Reflecting**

Homework Assignments

_____
_____
_____
_____
_____

Other Teaching Materials

_____
_____
_____
_____
_____

Narrative of the Life of Frederick Douglass **Pages 562–573**

Core Objectives
- Understand and appreciate a slave narrative
- Examine autobiography and style
- Analyze author's purpose

MISSOURI PLANNER
Grade-Level Expectations
R1.C, R1.D, R1.F, R1.G, R1.H, R1.I, R2.A, R2.B, R3.B, R2.C, W1.A, LS2.A, IL1.A, IL1.B, IL1.C

Integrating Skills

Grammar
- Identifying Clauses: Independent and Subordinate

Vocabulary
- Context Clues
- Connotation/Denotation

Preparing to Read
____ Connect to Your Life
____ Build Background
____ Vocabulary Preview: Using Context Clues   ❏ Unit Four Resource Book: Words to Know SkillBuilder, p. 7
____ Focus Your Reading
          Literary Analysis: Autobiography and Style   ❏ Unit Four Resource Book: Literary Analysis SkillBuilder, p. 6
          Active Reading: Author's Purpose   ❏ Unit Four Resource Book: Active Reading SkillBuilder, p. 5

Teaching the Literature   ❏ PE pp. 562–573
____ Reading the Selection   ❏ Unit Four Resource Book: Summary, p. 4

Thinking Through the Literature
____ Connect to the Literature
____ Think Critically   ❏ Reading and Critical Thinking Transparencies, T19
____ Extend Interpretations
____ Literary Analysis: Autobiography and Style   ❏ Literary Analysis Transparencies, T23

Choices and Challenges

Writing Options
____ Closing Statement
____ Antislavery Editorial
____ Comparison of Slave Narratives
____ Autobiographical Sketch

Activities and Explorations
____ Living to Tell
____ Story in Pictures
____ Discussion of Covey

Inquiry and Research
____ Another View
____ Slave Laws

Narrative of the Life of Frederick Douglass

Choices and Challenges (continued)
Vocabulary in Action
____ Meaning Clues

Author Activity
____ Poetic Tribute
____ Art Connection

Teaching Options (from Teacher's Edition)
Mini Lessons

Preteaching Vocabulary
____ Using Context Clues

Vocabulary Strategy
____ Connotation/Denotation   ❏ Vocabulary Transparencies and Copymasters, C49

Grammar
____ Identifying Clauses: Independent and   ❏ Grammar Transparencies and Copymasters, C88
Subordinate

Speaking and Listening
____ Persuasive Speech

Viewing and Representing
Art Appreciation
____ *Head of a Negro* by John Singleton Copley

Cross Curricular Link
____ History

Informal Assessment
____ Summarizing

Assessment
____ Selection Quiz   ❏ Unit Four Resource Book: Selection Quiz, p. 8
____ Selection Test   ❏ Formal Assessment: Selection Test, p. 105–106
____ Test Generator

Homework Assignments
_____
_____
_____
_____
_____

Other Teaching Materials
_____
_____
_____
_____
_____

Stanzas on Freedom / Free Labor

Core Objectives
- Understand and appreciate protest poems that explore the meaning of freedom and slavery
- Identify and appreciate symbols in a poem
- Apply strategies for reading protest poetry

MISSOURI PLANNER
Grade-Level Expectations
R1.C, R1.D, R1.F, R1.G, R1.H, R1.I, R2.A, R2.C, W1.A

Integrating Skills
Grammar
- Clauses vs. Phrases

Vocabulary
- Understanding Figurative Language Through Context

Preparing to Read
____ Connect to Your Life
____ Build Background
____ Focus Your Reading
     Literary Analysis: Symbol   ❑ Unit Four Resource Book: Literary Analysis SkillBuilder, p. 10
     Active Reading: Strategies for Reading   ❑ Unit Four Resource Book: Active Reading SkillBuilder, p. 9
       Protest Poetry

Teaching the Literature
____ Reading the Selection   ❑ PE pp. 574–579

Thinking Through the Literature
____ Connect to the Literature
____ Think Critically
____ Extend Interpretations
____ Literary Analysis: Symbol

Choices and Challenges
Writing Options
____ New Stanza
____ Protest Poem

Activities and Explorations
____ Political Poster

Stanzas on Freedom / Free Labor

Teaching Options (from Teacher's Edition)

Mini Lessons

Vocabulary Strategy

____ Understanding Figurative Language Through Context   ❑ Vocabulary Transparencies and Copymasters, C50

Grammar

____ Clauses vs. Phrases   ❑ Grammar Transparencies and Copymasters, C90

Speaking and Listening

____ Dramatic Reading

Informal Assessment

____ Contrasting Across Texts

Assessment

____ Selection Test   ❑ Formal Assessment: Selection Test, pp. 107–108

____ Test Generator

Homework Assignments

_____

_____

_____

_____

_____

Other Teaching Materials

_____

_____

_____

_____

_____

An Occurrence at Owl Creek Bridge

Core Objectives
- Appreciate a short story about the Civil War
- Identify and examine point of view
- Analyze structure in a short story

> **MISSOURI PLANNER**
> Grade-Level Expectations
> R1.C, R1.D, R1.F, R1.G, R1.H, R1.I, R2.A, R2.C, W1.A

Integrating Skills

Grammar
- Essential vs. Nonessential Clauses
- Punctuation for Clauses

Vocabulary
- Context Clues
- Applying Meaning of Prefixes

Preparing to Read
____ Connect to Your Life
____ Build Background
____ Vocabulary Preview: Using Context Clues   ❏ Unit Four Resource Book: Words to Know SkillBuilder, p. 14
____ Focus Your Reading
     Literary Analysis: Point of View   ❏ Unit Four Resource Book: Literary Analysis SkillBuilder, p. 13
     Active Reading: Analyzing Structure   ❏ Unit Four Resource Book: Active Reading SkillBuilder, p. 12

Teaching the Literature
                                      ❏ PE pp. 580–592
____ Reading the Selection   ❏ Unit Four Resource Book: Summary, p. 11

Thinking Through the Literature
____ Connect to the Literature
____ Think Critically   ❏ Reading and Critical Thinking Transparencies, T6, T17
____ Extend Interpretations
____ Literary Analysis: Point of View   ❏ Literary Analysis Transparencies, T20

Choices and Challenges
Writing Options
____ Evaluation of Bierce
____ Comparison Essay

Vocabulary in Action
____ Synonyms

An Occurrence at Owl Creek Bridge

Teaching Options (from Teacher's Edition)

Mini Lessons

Preteaching Vocabulary
____ Using Context Clues

Vocabulary Strategy
____ Applying Meanings of Prefixes   ❏ Vocabulary Transparencies and Copymasters, C51

Grammar
____ Essential vs. Nonessential Clauses   ❏ Grammar Transparencies and Copymasters, T44, C91
____ Punctuation for Clauses   ❏ Grammar Transparencies and Copymasters, T55, C149

Speaking and Listening
____ Realistic Dialogue

Viewing and Representing
Art Appreciation
____ *Union Soldiers* by anonymous
____ Story Illustrations

Cross Curricular Link

History
____ The 54th Regiment

Informal Assessment
____ Self-Assessment

Assessment
____ Selection Quiz   ❏ Unit Four Resource Book: Selection Quiz, p. 15
____ Selection Test   ❏ Formal Assessment: Selection Test, pp. 109–110
____ Test Generator

Homework Assignments

_____
_____
_____
_____
_____

Other Teaching Materials

_____
_____
_____
_____
_____

A Mystery of Heroism

Core Objectives

- Understand and appreciate a short story
- Identify characteristics of naturalism in the story
- Visualize the setting, characters, and events in the story

MISSOURI PLANNER
Grade-Level Expectations
R1.C, R1.D, R1.F, R1.G, R1.H, R1.I, R2.A, R2.B, R2.C, W1.A, IL1.A, IL1.B, IL1.C

Integrating Skills

Grammar

- Introduction to Adjective Clauses
- Use of Commas in Names and Titles

Vocabulary

- Using Context Clues
- Root Words

Preparing to Read

____ Connect to Your Life
____ Build Background
____ Vocabulary Preview: Using Context Clues   ❏ Unit Four Resource Book: Words to Know SkillBuilder, p. 19
____ Focus Your Reading
     Literary Analysis: Naturalism   ❏ Unit Four Resource Book: Literary Analysis SkillBuilder, p. 18
     Active Reading: Visualizing   ❏ Unit Four Resource Book: Active Reading SkillBuilder, p. 17

Teaching the Literature

     ❏ PE pp. 593–604
____ Reading the Selection   ❏ Unit Four Resource Book: Summary, p. 16

Thinking Through the Literature

____ Connect to the Literature
____ Think Critically   ❏ Reading and Critical Thinking Transparencies, T8
____ Extend Interpretations
____ Literary Analysis: Naturalism

Choices and Challenges

Writing Options

____ Letter Home
____ Literary Analysis
____ Different Ending

Activities and Explorations

____ Combat Sketch
____ War Songs
____ Interview with Collins

Inquiry and Research

____ Photo Gallery

Vocabulary in Action

____ Meaning Clues

Author Activity

____ War Stories

A Mystery of Heroism

Teaching Options (from Teacher's Edition)

Mini Lessons

Preteaching Vocabulary
____ Using Context Clues

Vocabulary Strategy
____ Root Words ❏ Vocabulary Transparencies and Copymasters, C52

Grammar
____ Introduction to Adjective Clauses ❏ Grammar Transparencies and Copymasters, C92
____ Use of Commas in Names and Titles ❏ Grammar Transparencies and Copymasters, C150

Speaking and Listening
____ Persuasive Speaking

Viewing and Representing
Art Appreciation
____ *The Battle of Chancellorsville*
by unknown artist

Cross Curricular Link

History
____ Parallel Naturalist Movements in Other Cultures

Informal Assessment

____ Identifying Supporting Ideas

Assessment

____ Selection Quiz ❏ Unit Four Resource Book: Selection Quiz, p. 20
____ Selection Test ❏ Formal Assessment: Selection Test, pp. 111–112
____ Test Generator

Homework Assignments

_____
_____
_____
_____
_____

Other Teaching Materials

_____
_____
_____
_____
_____

The Gettysburg Address

Core Objectives
- Understand and appreciate a classic speech
- Identify and examine style in a speech
- Appreciate historical context in a speech

```
┌─────────────────────────────────────┐
│         MISSOURI PLANNER             │
│      Grade-Level Expectations        │
│  R1.C, R1.D, R1.E, R1.F, R1.G, R1.H, R1.I, R2.A, │
│  R2.C, W1.A, IL1.A, IL1.B, IL1.C     │
└─────────────────────────────────────┘
```

Integrating Skills

Grammar
- Adjective and Relative Clauses

Vocabulary
- Context Clues

Preparing to Read
____ Connect to Your Life
____ Build Background
____ Vocabulary Preview: Using Context Clues   ❑ Unit Four Resource Book: Words to Know SkillBuilder, p. 24
____ Focus Your Reading
         Literary Analysis: Style   ❑ Unit Four Resource Book: Literary Analysis SkillBuilder, p. 23
         Active Reading: Interpreting Historical Context ❑ Unit Four Resource Book: Active Reading SkillBuilder, p. 22

Teaching the Literature   ❑ PE pp. 605–608
____ Reading the Selection   ❑ Unit Four Resource Book: Summary, p. 21

Thinking Through the Literature
____ Connect to the Literature
____ Think Critically   ❑ Reading and Critical Thinking Transparency, T41
____ Extend Interpretations
____ Literary Analysis: Style   ❑ Literary Analysis Transparencies, T23

Choices and Challenges

Writing Options
____ Modern Paraphrase
____ Letter to Lincoln

Inquiry and Research
____ Battle Report

Vocabulary in Action
____ Context Clues

The Gettysburg Address

Teaching Options (from Teacher's Edition)

Mini Lesson

Preteaching Vocabulary
____ Using Context Clues

Grammar
____ Adjective and Relative Clauses ❑ Grammar Transparencies and Copymasters, T44, C95

Assessment
____ Selection Quiz ❑ Unit Four Resource Book: Selection Quiz, p. 25
____ Selection Test ❑ Formal Assessment: Selection Test, pp. 113–114
____ Test Generator

Homework Assignments

_____
_____
_____
_____
_____

Other Teaching Materials

_____
_____
_____
_____
_____

Coming of Age in Mississippi

Core Objectives
- Appreciate a selection from an autobiography
- Understand an eyewitness report
- Use chronological order to understand an eyewitness report

> **MISSOURI PLANNER**
> Grade-Level Expectations
> R1.C, R1.D, R1.F, R1.G, R1.H, R1.I, R2.A, R2.C, W1.A, W3.C

Integrating Skills

Grammar
- Adverb Clauses
- Punctuation of Adverb Clauses

Vocabulary
- Sensory Details

Preparing to Read
___ Connect to Your Life
___ Build Background
___ Focus Your Reading
    Literary Analysis: Eyewitness Report   ❑ Unit Four Resource Book: Literary Analysis SkillBuilder, p. 28
    Active Reading: Chronological Order   ❑ Unit Four Resource Book: Active Reading SkillBuilder, p. 27

Teaching the Literature
        ❑ PE pp. 609–617
___ Reading the Selection   ❑ Unit Four Resource Book: Summary, p. 26

Thinking Through the Literature
___ Connect to the Literature
___ Think Critically   ❑ Reading and Critical Thinking Transparencies, T17, T49
___ Extend Interpretations
___ Literary Analysis: Eyewitness Report   ❑ Literary Analysis Transparencies, T16

Choices and Challenges

Writing Options
___ Mother's Letter, Anne's Reply
___ Points of Comparison
___ Eyewitness Account

Activities and Explorations
___ On the Scene

Art Connection
___ Under Siege

___ **Author Activity**

Coming of Age in Mississippi

Teaching Options (from Teacher's Edition)

Mini Lessons

Vocabulary Strategy

____ Sensory Details

❑ Vocabulary Transparencies and Copymasters, C53

Grammar

____ Adverb Clauses

❑ Grammar Transparencies and Copymasters, C96

____ Punctuation of Adverb Clauses

❑ Grammar Transparencies and Copymasters, C151

Viewing and Representing

Art Appreciation

____ Photograph

Cross Curricular Link

____ History

Informal Assessment

____ Literary Response

Assessment

____ Selection Quiz

❑ Unit Four Resource Book: Selection Quiz, p. 29

____ Selection Test

❑ Formal Assessment: Selection Test, pp. 115–116

____ Test Generator

Homework Assignments

_____

_____

_____

_____

Other Teaching Materials

_____

_____

_____

_____

Ballad of Birmingham

Core Objectives
- Understand and appreciate a ballad commemorating a tragic event
- Identify and appreciate the characteristics of ballads
- Apply strategies for reading narrative poetry

Integrating Skills
Grammar
- Introduction to Noun Clauses

```
MISSOURI PLANNER
Grade-Level Expectations
R1.C, R1.D, R1.F, R1.G, R1.H, R1.I, R2.A, R2.C,
W1.A, IL1.A, IL1.B, IL1.C
```

Preparing to Read
____ Connect to Your Life
____ Build Background
____ Focus Your Reading
     Literary Analysis: Ballads   ❑ Unit Four Resource Book: Literary Analysis SkillBuilder, p. 31
     Active Reading: Reading Narrative Poetry   ❑ Unit Four Resource Book: Active Reading SkillBuilder, p. 30

Teaching the Literature
____ Reading the Selection   ❑ PE pp. 618–621

Thinking Through the Literature
____ Connect to the Literature
____ Think Critically   ❑ Reading and Critical Thinking Transparencies, T5
____ Extend Interpretations
____ Literary Analysis: Ballads

Choices and Challenges
Writing Options
____ Original Ballad
____ Points of Comparison

Activities and Explorations
____ Learned By Heart
____ Sorrowful Song
____ Ballads of Today

Inquiry and Research
____ Events in Birmingham

____ **Author Activity**

Teaching Options (from Teacher's Edition)

Mini Lessons

Grammar

____ Introduction to Noun Clauses ❑ Grammar Transparencies and Copymasters, C101

Informal Assessment

____ Identifying Theme

Assessment

____ Selection Test

____ Part Test

____ Test Generator

❑ Unit Four Resource Book: Selection Quiz, p. 117

❑ Formal Assessment: Unit Four, Part 1 Test, pp. 119–120

Homework Assignments

_____

_____

_____

_____

_____

Other Teaching Materials

_____

_____

_____

_____

_____

Literary Interpretation

Writing Prompt
Write an interpretation of a literary work
in which you explain its meaning.

> **MISSOURI PLANNER**
> Grade-Level Expectations
> R3.D, W1.A, W2.D, W2.F, W3.C

Preparing to Read

____ Introduction
____ Basics in a Box
____ Using the Graphic

❑ Writing Transparencies and Copymasters, T11, T20, C30

____ Analyzing a Student Model
"The Red Badge of Courage"

❑ Unit Four Resource Book: Student Models, pp. 38–43

Writing

____ **Prewriting**
Choosing a Literary Work
Planning the Literary Interpretation

❑ Unit Four Resource Book: Prewriting, p. 33

____ **Drafting**
Organizing the Draft

❑ Unit Four Resource Book: Drafting and Elaboration, p. 34

____ **Peer Review**
Ask Your Peer Reader

❑ Unit Four Resource Book: Peer Response Guide, pp. 35–36

____ **Revising**
Conclusions

❑ Unit Four Resource Book: Revising, Editing, and Proofreading, p. 37
❑ Unit Four Resource Book: Rubric for Evaluation, p. 44

____ **Editing and Proofreading**
Verb Tense

____ **Reflecting**

Homework Assignments

_____
_____
_____
_____
_____

Other Teaching Materials

_____
_____
_____
_____
_____

The Indian and the Hundred Cows /
El indito de las cien vacas

Core Objectives
- Understand and appreciate a *cuento,* or a folk tale
- Identify characteristics of *cuentos*
- Determine the theme of a *cuento*

> **MISSOURI PLANNER**
> Grade-Level Expectations
> R1.C, R1.D, R1.F, R1.G, R1.H, R1.I, R2.A, R2.C,
> W1.A, IL1.A, IL1.B, IL1.C

Integrating Skills
Grammar
- Independent and
  Subordinate Clauses

Vocabulary
- Using a Dictionary
  to Determine Usage

Preparing to Read
____ Connect to Your Life
____ Build Background
____ Focus Your Reading
　　　Literary Analysis: Cuento
　　　Active Reading: Determining Theme

❏ Unit Four Resource Book: Literary Analysis SkillBuilder, p. 49
❏ Unit Four Resource Book: Active Reading SkillBuilder, p. 48

Teaching the Literature
____ Reading the Selection

❏ PE pp. 638–644
❏ Unit Four Resource Book: Summary, p. 47

Thinking Through the Literature
____ Connect to the Literature
____ Think Critically
____ Extend Interpretations
____ Literary Analysis: Cuento

❏ Literary Analysis Transparencies, T24

Choices and Challenges
Writing Options
____ Sermon on Charity
____ Comic Tale

Activities and Explorations
____ Mural Art

Inquiry and Research
____ Translations from Spanish

The Indian and the Hundred Cows /
El indito de las cien vacas

Teaching Options (from Teacher's Edition)

Mini Lessons

Vocabulary Strategy

____ Using a Dictionary to Determine Usage ❑ Vocabulary Transparencies and Copymasters, C54

Grammar

____ Independent and Subordinate Clauses ❑ Grammar Transparencies and Copymasters, C89

Speaking and Listening

____ Telling Stories

Informal Assessment

____ Making a Judgment

Assessment

____ Selection Quiz ❑ Unit Four Resource Book: Selection Quiz, p. 50

____ Selection Test ❑ Formal Assessment: Selection Test, p. 121

____ Test Generator

Homework Assignments

_____

_____

_____

_____

_____

Other Teaching Materials

_____

_____

_____

_____

_____

High Horse's Courting *from* Black Elk Speaks   Pages 645–653

Core Objectives
- Appreciate a Sioux folk tale
- Understand and appreciate oral literature
- Identify author's purpose

MISSOURI PLANNER

Grade-Level Expectations

R1.C, R1.D, R1.F, R1.G, R1.H, R1.I, R2.A, R2.C, W1.A, IL1.A, IL1.B, IL1.C

Integrating Skills
Grammar
- Phrases and Clauses

Vocabulary
- Using Reference Materials

Preparing to Read
____ Connect to Your Life
____ Build Background
____ Focus Your Reading
     Literary Analysis: Oral Literature   ❑ Unit Four Resource Book: Literary Analysis SkillBuilder, p. 53
     Active Reading: Identifying Author's Purpose   ❑ Unit Four Resource Book: Active Reading SkillBuilder, p. 52

Teaching the Literature
                                        ❑ PE pp. 645–653
____ Reading the Selection   ❑ Unit Four Resource Book: Summary, p. 51

Thinking Through the Literature
____ Connect to the Literature
____ Think Critically   ❑ Reading and Critical Thinking Transparencies, T19
____ Extend Interpretations
____ Literary Analysis: Oral Literature

Choices and Challenges
Writing Options
____ Modernizing a Story

Activities and Explorations
____ Talk Show

Inquiry and Research
____ Sioux Culture

High Horse's Courting *from* Black Elk Speaks

Teaching Options (from Teacher's Edition)

Mini Lessons

Vocabulary Strategy
____ Using Reference Materials: Specialized Dictionaries

❑ Vocabulary Transparencies and Copymasters, C55

Grammar
____ Phrases and Clauses

❑ Grammar Transparencies and Copymasters, C90

Viewing and Representing
Art Appreciation
____ *Night Horse* by C. J. Wells

Cross Curricular Link

History
____ The Vanishing Frontier

Informal Assessment
____ Predicting Outcomes

Assessment
____ Selection Quiz
____ Selection Test
____ Test Generator

❑ Unit Four Resource Book: Selection Quiz, p. 54
❑ Formal Assessment: Selection Test, p. 123

Homework Assignments

_____
_____
_____
_____
_____

Other Teaching Materials

_____
_____
_____
_____
_____

from The Autobiography of Mark Twain

Core Objectives
- Understand and appreciate an autobiography
- Identify and understand irony
- Predict events in an autobiography

MISSOURI PLANNER
Grade-Level Expectations
R1.C, R1.D, R1.F, R1.G, R1.H, R1.I, R2.A, R2.C, W1.A, IL1.A, IL1.B, IL1.C

Integrating Skills

Grammar
- Essential vs. Nonessential Clauses
- Punctuating Clauses in a Series

Vocabulary
- Using Context Clues
- Identifying Synonyms and Antonyms

Preparing to Read
____ Connect to Your Life
____ Build Background
____ Vocabulary Preview: Using Context Clues   ❑ Unit Four Resource Book: Words to Know SkillBuilder, p. 58
____ Focus Your Reading
    Literary Analysis: Irony   ❑ Unit Four Resource Book: Literary Analysis SkillBuilder, p. 57
    Active Reading: Predicting   ❑ Unit Four Resource Book: Active Reading SkillBuilder, p. 56

Teaching the Literature
❑ PE pp. 658–668
____ Reading the Selection   ❑ Unit Four Resource Book: Summary, p. 55

Thinking Through the Literature
____ Connect to the Literature
____ Think Critically   ❑ Reading and Critical Thinking Transparencies, T2
____ Extend Interpretations
____ Literary Analysis: Irony

Choices and Challenges
Writing Options
____ Screenplay Script
____ Instruction Manual
____ Newspaper Report

Activities and Explorations
____ Stage Directions
____ Advertising Flyer

Inquiry and Research
____ Science

Vocabulary in Action
____ Assessment Practice

from The Autobiography of Mark Twain

Teaching Options (from Teacher's Edition)

Mini Lessons

Preteaching Vocabulary
____ Using Context Clues

Vocabulary Strategy
____ Identifying Synonyms and Antonyms   ❏ Vocabulary Transparencies and Copymasters, C56

Grammar
____ Essential vs. Nonessential Clauses   ❏ Grammar Transparencies and Copymasters, T55, C91
____ Punctuating Clauses in a Series   ❏ Grammar Transparencies and Copymasters, C156

Speaking and Listening
____ Storytelling

Viewing and Representing
Art Appreciation
____ *Untitled*

Inquiry and Research
____ Using Indexes

Informal Assessment
____ Point of View

Assessment
____ Selection Quiz   ❏ Unit Four Resource Book: Selection Quiz, p. 59
____ Selection Test   ❏ Formal Assessment: Selection Test, pp. 125–126
____ Test Generator

Homework Assignments

_____

_____

_____

_____

_____

Other Teaching Materials

_____

_____

_____

_____

_____

from Life on the Mississippi

Core Objectives
- Appreciate a selection from a classic memoir
- Appreciate and examine description
- Visualize details in a memoir

MISSOURI PLANNER

Grade-Level Expectations

R1.C, R1.D, R1.F, R1.G, R1.H, R1.I, R2.A, R2.C, W1.A, LS2.A, IL1.A, IL1.B, IL1.C, IL.2.A

Integrating Skills

Grammar	Vocabulary
■ Adjective Clauses	■ Analogies
■ Commas with Names and Titles	
■ Double Negatives	

Preparing to Read
___ Connect to Your Life
___ Build Background
___ Focus Your Reading
      Literary Analysis: Description   ❑ Unit Four Resource Book: Literary Analysis SkillBuilder, p. 62
      Active Reading: Visualizing   ❑ Unit Four Resource Book: Active Reading SkillBuilder, p. 61

Teaching the Literature
     ❑ PE pp. 669–677
___ Reading the Selection   ❑ Unit Four Resource Book: Summary, p. 60

Thinking Through the Literature
___ Connect to the Literature
___ Think Critically   ❑ Reading and Critical Thinking Transparencies, T8
___ Extend Interpretations
___ Literary Analysis: Description

Choices and Challenges

Writing Options
___ Diary Entry
___ Magazine Article

Activities and Explorations
___ Occupational Outlook
___ Video Adaptation

Inquiry and Research
___ Geography

from Life on the Mississippi

Teaching Options (from Teacher's Edition)

Mini Lessons

Vocabulary Strategy
____ Understanding Analogies ❑ Vocabulary Transparencies and Copymasters, C57

Grammar
____ Introductory Words for Adjective ❑ Grammar Transparencies and Copymasters, T44, C94
Clauses
____ Commas in Names and Titles ❑ Grammar Transparencies and Copymasters, C150

Speaking and Listening
____ Persuading

Cross Curricular Link

Workplace
____ Starting a New Job

Informal Assessment
____ Story Extension

Assessment
____ Selection Quiz ❑ Unit Four Resource Book: Selection Quiz, p. 63
____ Selection Test ❑ Formal Assessment: Selection Test, pp. 127–128
____ Test Generator

Homework Assignments

_____
_____
_____
_____
_____

Other Teaching Materials

_____
_____
_____
_____
_____

The Notorious Jumping Frog
of Calaveras County

Pages 679–687

Core Objectives
- Understand and appreciate a classic short story
- Identify characteristics of a tall tale
- Understand Twain's use of dialect

```
┌─────────────────────────────────────────┐
│            MISSOURI PLANNER               │
│         Grade-Level Expectations          │
│  R1.C, R1.D, R1.E, R1.F, R1.G, R1.H, R1.I, R2.A, │
│  R2.C, W1.A                               │
└─────────────────────────────────────────┘
```

Integrating Skills

Grammar
- Use of *That* and *Which* in Adjective Clauses

Vocabulary
- Using Context Clues
- Applying Meanings of Root Words

Preparing to Read
____ Connect to Your Life
____ Build Background
____ Vocabulary Preview: Using Context Clues   ❑ Unit Four Resource Book: Words to Know SkillBuilder, p. 67
____ Focus Your Reading
      Literary Analysis: Tall Tale   ❑ Unit Four Resource Book: Literary Analysis SkillBuilder, p. 66
      Active Reading: Understanding Dialect   ❑ Unit Four Resource Book: Active Reading SkillBuilder, p. 65

Teaching the Literature
                                                   ❑ PE pp. 679–687
____ Reading the Selection   ❑ Unit Four Resource Book: Summary, p. 64

Thinking Through the Literature
____ Connect to the Literature
____ Think Critically
____ Extend Interpretations
____ Literary Analysis: Tall Tale
____ Author's Style

Choices and Challenges

Writing Options
____ The Stranger's Tale
____ Local Storytelling
____ Dialects Today

Vocabulary in Action
____ Meaning Clues
____ Word Knowledge

____ **Author Study Project**

The Notorious Jumping Frog
of Calaveras County

Teaching Options (from Teacher's Edition)

Mini Lessons

Preteaching Vocabulary
____ Using Context Clues

Vocabulary Strategy
____ Applying Meanings of Root Words

❑ Vocabulary Transparencies and Copymasters, C58

Grammar
____ Use of *That* and *Which* in Adjective
Clauses

❑ Grammar Transparencies and Copymasters, T44, C93

Speaking and Listening
____ Telling a Humorous Anecdote

Viewing and Representing
____ Analyzing a Performance Review

Cross Curricular Link

Multicultural
____ Tall Tales of the 20th Century

Informal Assessment
____ Letter Writing

Assessment
____ Selection Quiz
____ Selection Test
____ Test Generator

❑ Unit Four Resource Book: Selection Quiz, p. 68
❑ Formal Assessment: Selection Test, pp. 129–130

Homework Assignments

_____
_____
_____
_____
_____

Other Teaching Materials

_____
_____
_____
_____
_____

A Wagner Matinee

Core Objectives
- Understand and appreciate a short story
- Identify and understand setting
- Draw conclusions about character in a short story

> **MISSOURI PLANNER**
> Grade-Level Expectations
> R1.C, R1.D, R1.E, R1.F, R1.G, R1.H, R1.I, R2.A, R2.C, W1.A, IL1.A, IL1.B, IL1.C

Integrating Skills

Grammar
- Introductory Adverbial Clauses
- Punctuating Introductory Adverbial Clauses

Vocabulary
- Applying Meanings of Root Words

Preparing to Read
____ Connect to Your Life
____ Build Background
____ Vocabulary Preview: Applying Meanings   ❑ Unit Four Resource Book: Words to Know SkillBuilder, p. 72
      of Root Words
____ Focus Your Reading
      Literary Analysis: Setting   ❑ Unit Four Resource Book: Literary Analysis SkillBuilder, p. 71
      Active Reading: Drawing Conclusions   ❑ Unit Four Resource Book: Active Reading SkillBuilder, p. 70
          About Character

Teaching the Literature   ❑ PE pp. 688–699
____ Reading the Selection   ❑ Unit Four Resource Book: Summary, p. 69

Thinking Through the Literature
____ Connect to the Literature
____ Think Critically   ❑ Reading and Critical Thinking Transparencies, T1, T4, T39
____ Extend Interpretations
____ Literary Analysis: Setting   ❑ Literary Analysis Transparencies, T14

Choices and Challenges
Writing Options
____ Cause-and-Effect Analysis
____ Telegram from Boston
____ Interview: Personal Sacrifices

Activities and Explorations
____ Real Estate Ad
____ Opera Poster

Inquiry and Research
____ Music Appreciation

Vocabulary in Action
____ Context Clues

Author Activity
Willa Cather

A Wagner Matinee

Teaching Options (from Teacher's Edition)

Mini Lessons

Preteaching Vocabulary
____ Applying Meanings of Root Words

Grammar
____ Introductory Adverbial Clauses
____ Punctuating Introductory Adverbial Clauses

❏ Grammar Transparencies and Copymasters, C98
❏ Grammar Transparencies and Copymasters, C152

Viewing and Representing
Art Appreciation
____ *Mrs. Stewart, Housewife and Singer, Brasstown, North Carolina* by Doris Ulmann
____ *The Opera, Paris* by Raoul Dufy

Cross Curricular Links

History
____ Pioneer Families

Humanities
____ Music Appreciation

Informal Assessment
____ Write the Sequel

Assessment
____ Selection Quiz
____ Selection Test
____ Test Generator

❏ Unit Four Resource Book: Selection Quiz, p. 73
❏ Formal Assessment: Selection Test, pp. 131–132

Homework Assignments
_____
_____
_____
_____
_____

Other Teaching Materials
_____
_____
_____
_____
_____

The Legend of Gregorio Cortez

Core Objectives
- Appreciate a prose retelling of a traditional ballad
- Understand and appreciate a legend
- Make judgments about text

Integrating Skills

Grammar	Vocabulary
■ Introductory Words for Noun Clauses	■ Word History ■ English from Spanish

> **MISSOURI PLANNER**
> Grade-Level Expectations
> R1.C, R1.D, R1.F, R1.G, R1.H, R1.I, R2.A, R2.C,
> W1.A, IL1.A, IL1.B, IL1.C

Preparing to Read
____ Comparing Literature
____ Build Background
____ Focus Your Reading
    Literary Analysis: Legend   ❑ Unit Four Resource Book: Literary Analysis SkillBuilder, p. 76
    Active Reading: Making Judgments   ❑ Unit Four Resource Book: Active Reading SkillBuilder, p. 75
      About Text

Teaching the Literature
                                     ❑ PE pp. 702–719
____ Reading the Selection   ❑ Unit Four Resource Book: Summary, p. 74

Thinking Through the Literature
____ Connect to the Literature
____ Think Critically   ❑ Reading and Critical Thinking Transparencies, T5
____ Extend Interpretations
____ Literary Analysis: Legend   ❑ Literary Analysis Transparencies, T24

Choices and Challenges
Writing Options
____ Farewell Letter
____ Points of Comparison

Activities and Explorations
____ Map of the Setting
____ TV Newscast

Inquiry and Research
____ Colorful Folk Songs

Author Activity
____ The Storyteller's Voice

The Legend of Gregorio Cortez

Teaching Options (from Teacher's Edition)

Mini Lessons

Vocabulary Strategy

____ Word History   ❑ Vocabulary Transparencies and Copymasters, C60

____ English from Spanish   ❑ Vocabulary Transparencies and Copymasters, C61

Grammar

____ Introductory Words for Noun Clauses   ❑ Grammar Transparencies and Copymasters, T44, C104

Viewing and Representing

Art Appreciation

____ *Chama Running Red* by John Sloan

____ *Cliffs, Beyond Abiquiu, Dry Waterfall*
by Georgia O'Keefe

Cross Curricular Links

History

____ Texas Germans

____ Texas Rangers

Multicultural

____ Outlaw Heroes

____ Drawing from the Bible

Geography

____ Texas Geography

Government

____ Constitutional Law

Workplace Literacy

____ Writing Instructions

Informal Assessment

____ Character Clusters

Assessment

____ Selection Quiz   ❑ Unit Four Resource Book: Selection Quiz, p. 77

____ Selection Test   ❑ Formal Assessment: Selection Test, pp. 133–134

____ Part Test   ❑ Formal Assessment: Unit Four, Part 2 Test, pp. 135–136

____ Test Generator

Homework Assignments

_____

_____

_____

Other Teaching Materials

_____

_____

_____

Storytelling

Writing Prompt:
Prepare a script or notes in which you plan
to tell a story. Then tell a story.

```
┌─────────────────────────────────────┐
│          MISSOURI PLANNER            │
│       Grade-Level Expectations       │
│   R3.D, W1.A, W2.D, W2.E, W2.F       │
└─────────────────────────────────────┘
```

Preparing to Read

____ Introduction
____ Basics in a Box
____ Using the Guidelines and Standards

____ Analyzing a Storytelling Script   ❑ Unit Four Resource Book: Student Models, p. 84
A Storyteller in Action
"The Warrior Maiden"

Writing

____ **Prewriting**   ❑ Unit Four Resource Book: Planning Your Performance, p. 79
Planning the Performance
Developing the Performance

____ **Drafting**
Developing your Script

____ **Practicing and Presenting**   ❑ Unit Four Resource Book: Preparing, Practicing, and Presenting, p. 80

____ **Peer Review**   ❑ Unit Four Resource Book: Peer Response Guide, pp. 81–82
Ask Your Peer Reader

____ **Refining Your Performance**   ❑ Unit Four Resource Book: Refining, p. 83
Evaluating Your Interpretive Choices   ❑ Unit Four Resource Book: Standards for Evaluation, p. 85

____ **Reflecting**

Homework Assignments

_____
_____
_____
_____
_____

Other Teaching Materials

_____
_____
_____
_____
_____

Selected Poems by Emily Dickinson

Core Objectives

- Understand and appreciate representative poems by Emily Dickinson
- Identify and appreciate figurative language
- Apply strategies for reading poetry

> **MISSOURI PLANNER**
> Grade-Level Expectations
> R1.C, R1.D, R1.F, R1.G, R1.H, R1.I, R2.A, R2.B, R2.C, W1.A, LS1.A, LS1.B, IL1.A, IL1.B, IL1.C

Integrating Skills

Grammar	Vocabulary
■ Adjective and Adverb Clauses	■ Denotative and Connotative Meanings

Preparing to Read

____ Connect to Your Life
____ Build Background
____ Focus Your Reading
    Literary Analysis: Figurative Language   ❑ Unit Five Resource Book: Literary Analysis SkillBuilder, p. 5
    Active Reading: Strategies for Reading Poetry   ❑ Unit Five Resource Book: Active Reading SkillBuilder, p. 4

Teaching the Literature

____ Reading the Selection   ❑ PE pp. 750–762

Thinking Through the Literature

____ Connect to the Literature
____ Think Critically   ❑ Reading and Critical Thinking Transparencies, T50
____ Extend Interpretations
____ Literary Analysis: Figurative Language   ❑ Literary Analysis Transparencies, T13

Choices and Challenges

Writing Options

____ Mini Poem
____ Comparison Contrast Essay

Activities and Explorations

____ Illustrated Poem
____ Video Adaptation

Inquiry and Research

____ Historical Connection

Author Activity

____ Presenting a Poetry Slam

Selected Poems by Emily Dickinson

Teaching Options (from Teacher's Edition)

Mini Lessons

Vocabulary Strategy

____ Denotative and Connotative Meanings   ❏ Vocabulary Transparencies and Copymasters, C62

Grammar

____ Adjective and Adverb Clauses   ❏ Grammar Transparencies and Copymasters, C100

Cross Curricular Link

Social Sciences

____ Women's Education in the 19th Century

Informal Assessment

____ Recognizing Poetic Form

____ Making Inferences

Assessment

____ Selection Test   ❏ Formal Assessment: Selection Test, pp. 137–138

____ Test Generator

Homework Assignments

_____

_____

_____

_____

_____

Other Teaching Materials

_____

_____

_____

_____

_____

The Yellow Wallpaper

Pages 765–781

Core Objectives
- Understand and appreciate a classic short story
- Examine first-person narrator in a short story
- Make inferences about the narrator

MISSOURI PLANNER
Grade-Level Expectations
R1.C, R1.D, R1.E, R1.F, R1.G, R1.H, R1.I, R2.A, R2.C, W1.A, IL1.A, IL1.B, IL1.C

Integrating Skills

Grammar
- Subject-Verb Agreement
- Sentence Fragments

Vocabulary
- Using Context Clues
- Word Origins

Preparing to Read
____ Connect to Your Life
____ Build Background
____ Vocabulary Preview: Using Context Clues   ❑ Unit Five Resource Book: Words to Know SkillBuilder, p. 9
____ Focus Your Reading
    Literary Analysis: First-Person Narrator   ❑ Unit Five Resource Book: Literary Analysis SkillBuilder, p. 8
    Active Reading: Making Inferences About   ❑ Unit Five Resource Book: Active Reading SkillBuilder, p. 7
    the Narrator

Teaching the Literature
   ❑ PE pp. 765–781
____ Reading the Selection   ❑ Unit Five Resource Book: Summary, p. 6

Thinking Through the Literature
____ Connect to the Literature
____ Think Critically   ❑ Reading and Critical Thinking Transparencies, T7
____ Extend Interpretations
____ Literary Analysis: First-Person Narrator   ❑ Literary Analysis Transparencies, T14

Choices and Challenges
Writing Options
____ Advertising Copy
____ Letter to Editor
____ Extend the Story

Activities and Explorations
____ Dramatic Scene
____ Wallpaper Design
____ Top Story

Inquiry and Research
____ Depression

Vocabulary in Action
____ Meaning Clues

The Yellow Wallpaper

Teaching Options (from Teacher's Edition)

Mini Lessons

Preteaching Vocabulary
____ Using Context Clues

Vocabulary Strategy
____ Word Origins

❑ Vocabulary Transparencies and Copymasters, C63

Grammar
____ Subject-Verb Agreement
____ Sentence Fragments

❑ Grammar Transparencies and Copymasters, T47, C108
❑ Grammar Transparencies and Copymasters, C124

Speaking and Listening
____ Dramatic Reading
____ Role Playing

Viewing and Representing
Art Appreciation
____ *A Woman Sewing in an Interior*
by Wilhelm Hammershøi
____ *Stairway* by Edward Hopper

Cross Curricular Link

Psychology
____ Depression

Informal Assessment
____ Story Log
____ Sentence Completion

Assessment
____ Selection Quiz
____ Selection Test
____ Test Generator

❑ Unit Five Resource Book: Selection Quiz, p. 10
❑ Formal Assessment: Selection Test, pp. 139–140

Homework Assignments

_____

_____

_____

_____

_____

Other Teaching Materials

_____

_____

_____

_____

_____

The Story of an Hour

Core Objectives
- Understand and appreciate a short story
- Identify and appreciate plot and conflict
- Use clues in the story to make predictions

> **MISSOURI PLANNER**
> Grade-Level Expectations
> R1.C, R1.D, R1.F, R1.G, R1.H, R1.I, R2.A, R2.C, W1.A, W3.C, IL.2.A

Integrating Skills

Grammar
- Reviewing Complete Sentences

Vocabulary
- Using Reference Sources

Preparing to Read
___ Connect to Your Life
___ Build Background
___ Focus Your Reading
    Literary Analysis: Plot   ❑ Unit Five Resource Book: Literary Analysis SkillBuilder, p. 13
    Active Reading: Predicting   ❑ Unit Five Resource Book: Active Reading SkillBuilder, p. 12

Teaching the Literature
     ❑ PE pp. 783–787
___ Reading the Selection   ❑ Unit Five Resource Book: Summary, p. 11

Thinking Through the Literature
___ Connect to the Literature
___ Think Critically   ❑ Reading and Critical Thinking Transparencies, T2
___ Extend Interpretations
___ Literary Analysis: Plot and Surprise Ending

Choices and Challenges

Writing Options
___ Husband's Monologue
___ Wife's Epitaph
___ Different Ending
___ Essay About Marriage

Activities and Explorations
___ Story and Video

Inquiry and Research
___ Depression

The Story of an Hour

Teaching Options (from Teacher's Edition)

Mini Lessons

Vocabulary Strategy

____ Using Reference Sources ❏ Vocabulary Transparencies and Copymasters, C64

Grammar

____ Reviewing Complete Sentences ❏ Grammar Transparencies and Copymasters, T42, C73

Informal Assessment

____ Storyboard

Assessment

____ Selection Quiz ❏ Unit Five Resource Book: Selection Quiz, p. 14

____ Selection Test ❏ Formal Assessment: Selection Test, pp. 141–142

____ Test Generator

Homework Assignments

_____

_____

_____

_____

_____

Other Teaching Materials

_____

_____

_____

_____

Seventeen Syllables

Core Objectives
- Appreciate a Japanese-American short story
- Examine a coming-of-age story
- Understand conflict

```
┌─────────────────────────────────────┐
│         MISSOURI PLANNER             │
│       Grade-Level Expectations       │
│ R1.C, R1.D, R1.E, R1.F, R1.G, R1.H, R1.I, R2.A, │
│ R2.C, W1.A                           │
└─────────────────────────────────────┘
```

Integrating Skills

Grammar
- Adverb Clauses
- Semicolons and Conjunctive Adverbs

Vocabulary
- Using Context Clues
- Idioms

Preparing to Read
____ Comparing Literature
____ Build Background
____ Vocabulary Preview: Using Context Clues: ☐ Unit Five Resource Book: Words to Know SkillBuilder, p. 18
Synonyms
____ Focus Your Reading
Literary Analysis: Coming-of-Age Story   ☐ Unit Five Resource Book: Literary Analysis SkillBuilder, p. 17
Active Reading: Understanding Conflicts   ☐ Unit Five Resource Book: Active Reading SkillBuilder, p. 16

Teaching the Literature
☐ PE pp. 788–801
____ Reading the Selection   ☐ Unit Five Resource Book: Summary, p. 15

Thinking Through the Literature
____ Connect to the Literature
____ Think Critically
____ Extend Interpretations
____ Literary Analysis: Coming-of-Age Story

Choices and Challenges
Writing Options
____ Points of Comparison
____ Character Sketch

Vocabulary in Action
____ Context Clues

Seventeen Syllables

Teaching Options (from Teacher's Edition)

Mini Lessons

Preteaching Vocabulary

____ Using Context Clues: Synonyms

Vocabulary Strategy

____ Using Context to Understand Idioms ❑ Vocabulary Transparencies and Copymasters, C65

Grammar

____ Adverb Clauses: Subordinating Clauses ❑ Grammar Transparencies and Copymasters, C97

____ Semicolons and Conjunctive Adverbs ❑ Grammar Transparencies and Copymasters, C157

Speaking and Listening

____ Problem Solving by Role-Playing

Viewing and Representing

Art Appreciation

____ *Consolation* by Ruth Gikow

____ *Japanese American Family in the 1930s*
by Russell Lee

____ *Returning Sails to Gyotoku* by Ichiryusai Hiroshige

Cross Curricular Link

Workplace

____ Reading Maps

Informal Assessment

____ Arranging Events in Sequence

____ Self-Assessment

Assessment

____ Selection Quiz ❑ Unit Five Resource Book: Selection Quiz, p. 19

____ Selection Test ❑ Formal Assessment: Selection Test, pp. 143–144

____ Test Generator

Homework Assignments

_____

_____

_____

_____

_____

Other Teaching Materials

_____

_____

_____

_____

_____

Adolescence—III

Core Objectives
- Understand and appreciate a modern poem
- Identify and appreciate imagery
- Visualize the images in a poem

```
┌─────────────────────────────────────┐
│           MISSOURI PLANNER           │
│        Grade-Level Expectations      │
│  R1.C, R1.D, R1.F, R1.G, R1.H, R1.I, R2.A, R2.C, │
│  W1.A                                │
└─────────────────────────────────────┘
```

Integrating Skills

Grammar
- Adverb Clauses

Vocabulary
- Researching Word Origins

Preparing to Read
___ Comparing Literature
___ Build Background
___ Focus Your Reading
    Literary Analysis: Imagery
    Active Reading: Visualizing

❑ Unit Five Resource Book: Literary Analysis SkillBuilder, p. 21
❑ Unit Five Resource Book: Active Reading SkillBuilder, p. 20

Teaching the Literature
___ Reading the Selection

❑ PE pp. 802–805

Thinking Through the Literature
___ Connect to the Literature
___ Think Critically
___ Extend Interpretations
___ Literary Analysis: Imagery

❑ Reading and Critical Thinking Transparencies, T8

Choices and Challenges

Writing Options
___ Points of Comparison
___ Rosie's Diary Entry
___ Write a Review

Activities and Explorations
___ Sketch
___ Oral Interpretation

Adolescence—III

Teaching Options (from Teacher's Edition)

Mini Lessons

Vocabulary Strategy

____ Researching Word Origins   ❑ Vocabulary Transparencies and Copymasters, C66

Grammar

____ Adverb Clauses

Assessment

____ Selection Test   ❑ Formal Assessment: Selection Test, pp. 145–146

____ Test Generator

Homework Assignments

_____

_____

_____

_____

_____

Other Teaching Materials

_____

_____

_____

_____

_____

I Stand Here Ironing

Core Objectives
- Understand and appreciate a short story
- Understand interior monologue
- Make judgments about character

+--+
| **MISSOURI PLANNER** |
| Grade-Level Expectations |
| R1.C, R1.D, R1.F, R1.G, R1.H, R1.I, R2.A, R2.B, |
| R2.C, W1.A, IL1.A, IL1.B, IL1.C |
+--+

Integrating Skills

Grammar
- Adverbial Clauses
  with *Because*

Vocabulary
- Using Context Clues
- Homonyms

Preparing to Read
____ Comparing Literature
____ Build Background
____ Vocabulary Preview: Using Context Clues   ❏ Unit Five Resource Book: Words to Know SkillBuilder, p. 25
____ Focus Your Reading
     Literary Analysis: Interior Monologue   ❏ Unit Five Resource Book: Literary Analysis SkillBuilder, p. 24
     Active Reading: Making Judgments   ❏ Unit Five Resource Book: Active Reading SkillBuilder, p. 23
       About Character

Teaching the Literature
     ❏ PE pp. 806–817
____ Reading the Selection   ❏ Unit Five Resource Book: Summary, p. 22

Thinking Through the Literature
____ Connect to the Literature
____ Think Critically   ❏ Reading and Critical Thinking Transparencies, T5, T15
____ Extend Interpretations
____ Literary Analysis: Interior Monologue

Choices and Challenges
Writing Options
____ Points of Comparison
____ Story Sequel
____ Response to Relationships
____ Emily's Interview

Activities and Explorations
____ Guidelines for Parents
____ Informal Discussion
____ Role Play

____ **Art Connection**

____ **Inquiry and Research**
____ Sibling Rivalry
____ Oral History

I Stand Here Ironing

Choices and Challenges (continued)

Vocabulary in Action
____ Meaning Clues

Teaching Options (from Teacher's Edition)

Mini Lessons

Preteaching Vocabulary
____ Using Context Clues   ❑ Vocabulary Transparencies and Copymasters, C67

Vocabulary Strategy
____ Homonyms

Grammar
____ Adverbial Clauses with *Because*   ❑ Grammar Transparencies and Copymasters, C99

Speaking and Listening
____ Interviews

Viewing and Representing
Art Appreciation
____ *Girl Skipping Rope* by Ben Shahn
____ *The Brown Sweater* by Raphael Soyer

Cross Curricular Link

History
____ Working Women During the Depression

Informal Assessment
____ Point of View
____ Choosing the Best Summary

Assessment
____ Selection Quiz   ❑ Unit Five Resource Book: Selection Quiz, p. 26
____ Selection Test   ❑ Formal Assessment: Selection Test, pp. 147–148
____ Part Test   ❑ Formal Assessment: Unit Five, Part 1 Test, pp. 149–150
____ Test Generator

Homework Assignments

_____

_____

_____

_____

_____

Other Teaching Materials

_____

_____

_____

_____

_____

Chicago / Lucinda Matlock

Core Objectives
- Appreciate two classic poems
- Identify and examine tone
- Synthesize details in poetry

```
┌──────────────────────────────────────┐
│            MISSOURI PLANNER            │
│         Grade-Level Expectations       │
│  R1.C, R1.D, R1.F, R1.G, R1.H, R1.I, R2.A, R2.C, │
│  W1.A                                  │
└──────────────────────────────────────┘
```

Integrating Skills

Grammar
- Noun Clauses

Vocabulary
- Denotation and Connotation

Preparing to Read
___ Connect to Your Life
___ Build Background
___ Focus Your Reading
  Literary Analysis: Tone   ❑ Unit Five Resource Book: Literary Analysis SkillBuilder, p. 29
  Active Reading: Synthesizing Details   ❑ Unit Five Resource Book: Active Reading SkillBuilder, p. 28

Teaching the Literature
___ Reading the Selection   ❑ PE pp. 824–829

Thinking Through the Literature
___ Connect to the Literature
___ Think Critically   ❑ Reading and Critical Thinking Transparencies, T16
___ Extend Interpretations
___ Literary Analysis: Tone   ❑ Literary Analysis Transparencies, T19

Choices and Challenges
Writing Options
___ Hometown Poems
___ Comparison-Contrast Essay

Chicago / Lucinda Matlock

Teaching Options (from Teacher's Edition)
Mini Lessons
Vocabulary Strategy
____ Discriminating Between Connotative and Denotative Meaning

❑ Vocabulary Transparencies and Copymasters, C68

Grammar
____ Noun Clauses

❑ Grammar Transparencies and Copymasters, C102

Viewing and Representing
Art Appreciation
____ *City Building* and *Country Dance* by Thomas Hart Benton

Assessment
____ Selection Test
____ Test Generator

❑ Formal Assessment: Selection Test, pp. 151–152

Homework Assignments

Other Teaching Materials

Richard Cory / Miniver Cheevy

Core Objectives
- Appreciate two narrative poems
- Understand characterization in narrative poetry
- Evaluate character in poetry

```
┌─────────────────────────────────────┐
│          MISSOURI PLANNER            │
│       Grade-Level Expectations       │
│  R1.C, R1.D, R1.F, R1.G, R1.H, R1.I, R2.A, R2.C,│
│  W1.A                                │
└─────────────────────────────────────┘
```

Integrating Skills

Grammar   **Vocabulary**
- Noun Clauses   - Idioms

Preparing to Read
____ Connect to Your Life
____ Build Background
____ Focus Your Reading
    Literary Analysis: Characterization in   ❑ Unit Five Resource Book: Literary Analysis SkillBuilder, p. 31
      Narrative Poetry
    Active Reading: Evaluating Character   ❑ Unit Five Resource Book: Active Reading SkillBuilder, p. 30

Teaching the Literature
____ Reading the Selection   ❑ PE pp. 830–834

Thinking Through the Literature
____ Connect to the Literature
____ Think Critically   ❑ Reading and Critical Thinking Transparencies, T15
____ Extend Interpretations
____ Literary Analysis: Characterization in Narrative   ❑ Literary Analysis Transparencies, T6
    Poetry

Choices and Challenges
Writing Options
____ Miniver's Monologue
____ Farewell Note
____ Interview Questions

Activities and Explorations
____ Musical Adaptation

____ **Author Activities**

Selection Lesson Plan (continued)

Richard Cory / Miniver Cheevy

Teaching Options (from Teacher's Edition)

Mini Lessons

Vocabulary Strategy

____ Rely on Context to Determine Meanings of Idioms   ❑ Vocabulary Transparencies and Copymasters, C69

Grammar

____ Noun Clause   ❑ Grammar Transparencies and Copymasters, C102

Informal Assessment

____ Identifying the Best Summary

Assessment

____ Selection Test   ❑ Formal Assessment: Selection Test, pp. 153–154

____ Test Generator

Homework Assignments

_____

_____

_____

_____

_____

Other Teaching Materials

_____

_____

_____

_____

_____

We Wear the Mask / Sympathy

Core Objectives
- Understand and appreciate two poems
- Identify and examine symbol in poetry
- Interpret symbols in poetry

<table>
<tr><td colspan="2">MISSOURI PLANNER</td></tr>
<tr><td colspan="2">Grade-Level Expectations</td></tr>
<tr><td colspan="2">R1.C, R1.D, R1.F, R1.G, R1.H, R1.I, R2.A, R2.C, W1.A</td></tr>
</table>

Integrating Skills

Grammar	Vocabulary
■ Appositive Clauses	■ Connotation

Preparing to Read
____ Connect to Your Life
____ Build Background
____ Focus Your Reading
     Literary Analysis: Symbols   ❏ Unit Five Resource Book: Literary Analysis SkillBuilder, p. 33
     Active Reading: Interpreting Symbols   ❏ Unit Five Resource Book: Active Reading SkillBuilder, p. 32

Teaching the Literature
____ Reading the Selection   ❏ PE pp. 835–839

Thinking Through the Literature
____ Connect to the Literature
____ Think Critically
____ Extend Interpretations
____ Literary Analysis: Symbols   ❏ Literary Analysis Transparencies, T19

Choices and Challenges
Writing Options
____ Narrative Sequel
____ Lyrics of a Songbird

Activities and Explorations
____ Personal Mask
____ Political Cartoon

____ **Author Activity**

We Wear the Mask / Sympathy

Teaching Options (from Teacher's Edition)

Mini Lessons

Vocabulary Strategy
___ Interpret Connotative Power of Words   ❏ Vocabulary Transparencies and Copymasters, C70

Grammar
___ Appositive Clauses   ❏ Grammar Transparencies and Copymasters, C105

Assessment

___ Selection Test   ❏ Formal Assessment: Selection Test, pp. 155–156
___ Test Generator

Homework Assignments	Other Teaching Materials
_____	_____
_____	_____
_____	_____
_____	_____
_____	

Winter Dreams

Core Objectives
- Understand and appreciate a short story
- Analyze characters
- Evaluate character

Integrating Skills

Grammar	Vocabulary
■ Punctuation: Semicolons	■ Using Context Clues
■ Noun Clauses	■ Applying Meanings of Root Words

MISSOURI PLANNER
Grade-Level Expectations
R1.C, R1.D, R1.F, R1.G, R1.H, R1.I, R2.A, R2.B, R2.C, W1.A, W3.E, IL1.A, IL1.B, IL1.C

Preparing to Read
____ Connect to Your Life
____ Build Background
____ Vocabulary Preview: Using Context Clues   ❏ Unit Five Resource Book: Words to Know SkillBuilder, p. 37
____ Focus Your Reading
     Literary Analysis: Characters   ❏ Unit Five Resource Book: Literary Analysis SkillBuilder, p. 36
     Active Reading: Evaluating Character   ❏ Unit Five Resource Book: Active Reading SkillBuilder, p. 35

Teaching the Literature
                                           ❏ PE pp. 840–862
____ Reading the Selection   ❏ Unit Five Resource Book: Summary, p. 34

Thinking Through the Literature
____ Connect to the Literature
____ Think Critically   ❏ Reading and Critical Thinking Transparencies, T55
____ Extend Interpretations
____ Literary Analysis: Characters   ❏ Literary Analysis Transparencies, T6

Choices and Challenges
Writing Options
____ Psychological Evaluation
____ Dexter's Résumé
____ Personal Lecture

Activities and Explorations
____ Illustrated Calendar

Inquiry and Research
____ Clothing Styles

Art Connection

Vocabulary in Action
____ Synonyms

Winter Dreams

Teaching Options (from Teacher's Edition)

Mini Lessons

Preteaching Vocabulary
____ Using Context Clues

Vocabulary Strategy
____ Applying Meanings of Root Words   ❏ Vocabulary Transparencies and Copymasters, C71

Grammar
____ Punctuation: Semicolons   ❏ Grammar Transparencies and Copymasters, C158
____ Noun Clauses   ❏ Grammar Transparencies and Copymasters, C103

Speaking and Listening
____ Historical Recordings
____ Dramatic Reading

Viewing and Representing
Art Appreciation
____ *Autoportrait* by Tamara de Lempicka
____ *The Shelton with Sunspots* by Georgia O'Keefe

Assessment Preparation
____ Point of View
____ Alternative Ending

Inquiry and Research
____ Using Indexes

Cross Curricular Links

Music
____ Roots of Jazz

History
____ Women After World War I

Social Studies
____ The Aftermath of World War I

Informal Assessment
____ Point of View
____ Alternative Ending

Assessment
____ Selection Quiz   ❏ Unit Five Resource Book: Selection Quiz, p. 38
____ Selection Test   ❏ Formal Assessment: Selection Test, pp. 157–158
____ Test Generator

Homework Assignments

Other Teaching Materials

America and I

Core Objectives
- Understand and appreciate a short story
- Identify the elements of style that create voice
- Understand analogies

MISSOURI PLANNER

Grade-Level Expectations

R1.C, R1.D, R1.E, R1.F, R1.G, R1.H, R1.I, R2.A, R2.C, W1.A

Integrating Skills

Grammar
- Commas: Introductory Words
- Noun Clauses: Common Introductory Words

Vocabulary
- Using Context Clues
- Suffixes and Root Words

Preparing to Read
____ Connect to Your Life
____ Vocabulary Preview: Using Context Clues   ❑ Unit Five Resource Book: Words to Know SkillBuilder, p. 42
____ Focus Your Reading
     Literary Analysis: Voice   ❑ Unit Five Resource Book: Literary Analysis SkillBuilder, p. 41
     Active Reading: Understanding Analogies   ❑ Unit Five Resource Book: Active Reading SkillBuilder, p. 40

Teaching the Literature
     ❑ PE pp. 863–874
____ Reading the Selection   ❑ Unit Five Resource Book: Summary, p. 39

Thinking Through the Literature
____ Connect to the Literature
____ Think Critically   ❑ Reading and Critical Thinking Transparencies, T15
____ Extend Interpretations
____ Literary Analysis: Voice   ❑ Literary Analysis Transparencies, T23

Choices and Challenges
Writing Options
____ Tips for Newcomers
____ Letter to Russia
____ Looking Back: A Memoir

Vocabulary in Action
____ Context Clues

America and I

Teaching Options (from Teacher's Edition)

Mini Lessons

Preteaching Vocabulary
____ Using Context Clues

Vocabulary Strategy
____ Suffixes and Root Words ☐ Vocabulary Transparencies and Copymasters, C72

Grammar
____ Commas: Introductory Words ☐ Grammar Transparencies and Copymasters, C104
____ Noun Clauses: Common Introductory ☐ Grammar Transparencies and Copymasters, C153
Words

Speaking and Listening
____ Yiddish Words

Viewing and Representing
Art Appreciation
____ Photographs

Cross Curricular Links

History
____ Triangle Shirtwaist Company

Workplace
____ Reaching a Compromise

Informal Assessment
____ Choosing the Best Summary

Assessment

____ Selection Quiz ☐ Unit Five Resource Book: Selection Quiz, p. 43
____ Selection Test ☐ Formal Assessment: Selection Test, pp. 159–160
____ Test Generator

Homework Assignments

_____
_____
_____
_____
_____

Other Teaching Materials

_____
_____
_____
_____
_____

In the American Society

Core Objectives
- Appreciate a contemporary short story
- Identify and examine structure
- Make inferences about motivations

Integrating Skills

Grammar
- Noun Clauses

Vocabulary
- Context Clues
- Word History

Preparing to Read
____ Build Background
____ Vocabulary Preview: Using Context Clues   ❏ Unit Five Resource Book: Words to Know SkillBuilder, p. 47
____ Focus Your Reading
   Literary Analysis: Structure   ❏ Unit Five Resource Book: Literary Analysis SkillBuilder, p. 46
   Active Reading: Making Inferences   ❏ Unit Five Resource Book: Active Reading SkillBuilder, p. 45
      About Motivation

Teaching the Literature
                                                         ❏ PE pp. 877–893
____ Reading the Selection   ❏ Unit Five Resource Book: Summary, p. 44

Thinking Through the Literature
____ Connect to the Literature
____ Think Critically   ❏ Reading and Critical Thinking Transparencies, T7
____ Extend Interpretations
____ Literary Analysis: Structure

Choices and Challenges

Writing Options
____ Points of Comparison
____ Argument About Assimilation
____ Critical Review

Vocabulary in Action
____ Assessment Practice
____ Meaning Clues

In the American Society

Teaching Options (from Teacher's Edition)

Mini Lessons

Preteaching Vocabulary
____ Using Context Clues

Vocabulary Strategy
____ Word History   ❑ Vocabulary Transparencies and Copymasters, C73

Grammar
____ Introductory Words for Noun Clauses—   ❑ Grammar Transparencies and Copymasters, C106
Who and *Whom*

Speaking and Listening
____ Mandarin

Viewing and Representing
Art Appreciation
____ *Diner Interior with Coffee Urns* by Ralph Goings
____ *The Splash* by David Hockney

Cross Curricular Link
____ Religions in China

Workplace Links
____ Participating as a Member of a Team
____ Government
____ Immigration Law

Informal Assessment
____ Missing Chapter
____ Narrator's Voice

Assessment
____ Selection Quiz   ❑ Unit Five Resource Book: Selection Quiz, p. 48
____ Selection Test   ❑ Formal Assessment: Selection Test, pp. 161–162
____ Test Generator

Homework Assignments

_____

_____

_____

_____

_____

Other Teaching Materials

_____

_____

_____

_____

_____

Defining the Grateful Gesture / Refugee Ship   Pages 894–899

Core Objectives
- Understand and appreciate two contemporary poems
- Understand how theme and title are related
- Draw conclusions about theme

<table>
<tr><td colspan="2">**MISSOURI PLANNER**</td></tr>
<tr><td colspan="2">Grade-Level Expectations</td></tr>
<tr><td colspan="2">R1.C, R1.D, R1.F, R1.G, R1.H, R1.I, R2.A, R2.C, W1.A, W3.C</td></tr>
</table>

Integrating Skills

Grammar	Vocabulary
■ Pronouns in Comparison	■ Analogies

Preparing to Read
____ Comparing Literature
____ Build Background
____ Focus Your Reading
Literary Analysis: Theme and Title   ❑ Unit Five Resource Book: Literary Analysis SkillBuilder, p. 50
Active Reading: Drawing Conclusions   ❑ Unit Five Resource Book: Active Reading SkillBuilder, p. 49
About Theme

Teaching the Literature
____ Reading the Selection   ❑ PE pp. 894–899

Thinking Through the Literature
____ Connect to the Literature
____ Think Critically   ❑ Reading and Critical Thinking Transparencies, T4, T57
____ Extend Interpretations
____ Literary Analysis: Theme and Title

Choices and Challenges
Writing Options
____ Points of Comparison
____ Review of Sapia's Language

Activities and Explorations
____ Musical Adaptation

Defining the Grateful Gesture / Refugee Ship

Teaching Options (from Teacher's Edition)

Mini Lessons

Vocabulary Strategy
____ Understanding Analogies   ❑   Vocabulary Transparencies and Copymasters, C74

Grammar
____ Pronouns in Comparison   ❑   Grammar Transparencies and Copymasters, C126

Viewing and Representing
Art Appreciation
____ *Analogia IV* by Victor Grippo

Informal Assessment
____ Open-Ended Reading Items

Assessment

____ Selection Test   ❑   Unit Five Resource Book: Selection Test, pp. 163–164
____ Part Test   ❑   Formal Assessment: Unit Five Part 2 Test, pp. 165–166
____ Test Generator

Homework Assignments

_____
_____
_____
_____
_____

Other Teaching Materials

_____
_____
_____
_____

Comparison-and-Contrast Essay

Writing Prompt

Write a comparison-and-contrast essay in which
you explore the similarities and differences
between two or more subjects that interest you.

MISSOURI PLANNER
Grade-Level Expectations
R3.D, W1.A, W2.B, W2.D, W2.E, W2.F, W3.C

Preparing to Read

____ Introduction

____ Basics in a Box

____ Using the Graphic

____ Analyzing a Student Model
"Antigua: Almost Paradise"

❑ Writing Transparencies and Copymasters, T11, T20, C31, C32

❑ Unit Five Resource Book: Student Models, pp. 57–62

Writing

____ **Prewriting**
Choosing a Subject
Planning the Comparison-and-Contrast Essay

❑ Unit Five Resource Book: Prewriting, p. 52

____ **Drafting**
Organizing the Draft

❑ Unit Five Resource Book: Drafting and Elaboration, p. 53

____ **Peer Review**
Ask Your Peer Reader

❑ Unit Five Resource Book: Peer Response Guide, pp. 54–55

____ **Revising**
Parallel Construction

❑ Unit Five Resource Book: Revising, Editing, and Proofreading, p. 56
❑ Unit Five Resource Book: Rubric for Evaluation, p. 63

____ **Editing and Proofreading**
Modifiers

____ **Reflecting**

Homework Assignments

_____

_____

_____

_____

_____

Other Teaching Materials

_____

_____

_____

_____

_____

Selected Poems by Langston Hughes

Core Objectives
- Understand and appreciate representative poems by Langston Hughes
- Identify and appreciate mood
- Detect rhythm in poetry

> **MISSOURI PLANNER**
> Grade-Level Expectations
> R1.C, R1.D, R1.F, R1.G, R1.H, R1.I, R2.A, R2.C, W1.A, IL1.A, IL1.B, IL1.C

Integrating Skills

Grammar
- Varying Sentence Structure

Vocabulary
- Understanding Syllabic Marks

Preparing to Read
___ Connect to Your Life
___ Build Background
___ Focus Your Reading
　　Literary Analysis: Mood　　❑ Unit Six Resource Book: Literary Analysis SkillBuilder, p. 5
　　Active Reading: Detecting Rhythm in Poetry　　❑ Unit Six Resource Book: Active Reading SkillBuilder, p. 4

Teaching the Literature
___ Reading the Selection　　❑ PE pp. 924–929

Thinking Through the Literature
___ Connect to the Literature
___ Think Critically
___ Extend Interpretations
___ Literary Analysis: Mood　　❑ Literary Analysis Transparencies, T18

Choices and Challenges

Writing Options
___ Congratulatory Letter
___ Musical Poem
___ Compare-Contrast Essay

Activities and Explorations
___ Oral Readings
___ Poem Illustration
___ Map of Harlem
___ Blues Adaptation

Inquiry and Research
___ The Blues

Selected Poems by Langston Hughes

Teaching Options

Mini Lessons

Vocabulary Strategy

____ Understanding Syllabic Marks   ❑ Vocabulary Transparencies and Copymasters, C75

Grammar

____ Varying Sentence Structure   ❑ Grammar Transparencies and Copymasters, C164

Viewing and Representing

Art Appreciation

____ *Black Manhattan* by Romare Bearden

Informal Assessment

____ Oral Reading

Assessment

____ Selection Test   ❑ Formal Assessment: Selection Test, pp. 167–168

____ Test Generator

Homework Assignments

_____

_____

_____

_____

_____

Other Teaching Materials

_____

_____

_____

_____

When the Negro Was in Vogue

Core Objectives
- Understand and appreciate an essay
- Identify tone
- Draw conclusions about author's perspective

```
┌─────────────────────────────────────┐
│          MISSOURI PLANNER            │
│       Grade-Level Expectations       │
│  R1.C, R1.D, R1.F, R1.G, R1.H, R1.I, R2.A, R2.C, │
│  W1.A, IL1.A, IL1.B, IL1.C, IL.2.A   │
└─────────────────────────────────────┘
```

Integrating Skills

Grammar
- Adverbial Elements

Vocabulary
- Using Context to Build Vocabulary

Preparing to Read
____ Connect to Your Life
____ Build Background
____ Focus Your Reading
____ Literary Analysis: Tone   ❑ Unit Six Resource Book: Literary Analysis SkillBuilder, p. 7
        Active Reading: Drawing Conclusions   ❑ Unit Six Resource Book: Active Reading SkillBuilder, p. 6
            About Author's Perspective

Teaching the Literature
____ Reading the Selection   ❑ PE pp. 932–939

Thinking Through the Literature
____ Connect to the Literature
____ Think Critically   ❑ Reading and Critical Thinking Transparencies, T4, T22
____ Extend Interpretations
____ Literary Analysis: Tone   ❑ Literary Analysis Transparencies, T19

Choices and Challenges

Writing Options
____ Autobiographical Essay
____ Documentary Plan

Activities and Explorations
____ Music of the 1920s
____ Do the Lindy

Inquiry and Research
____ The Harlem Renaissance

____ **Author Study Project**

When the Negro Was in Vogue

Teaching Options (from Teacher's Edition)

Mini Lessons

Vocabulary Strategy
____ Using Context to Build Vocabulary   ❑ Vocabulary Transparencies and Copymasters, C76

Grammar
____ Adverbial Elements   ❑ Grammar Transparencies and Copymasters, C140

Speaking and Listening
____ Nonverbal Communication

Cross Curricular Link

Music
____ Recordings of Blues and Jazz

Informal Assessment
____ Summary

Assessment
____ Selection Test   ❑ Formal Assessment: Selection Test, pp. 169–170
____ Test Generator

Homework Assignments

_____

_____

_____

_____

_____

Other Teaching Materials

_____

_____

_____

_____

My City / Any Human to Another

Core Objectives
■ Understand and appreciate two sonnets
■ Determine major ideas in a poem

Integrating Skills

Grammar
■ Modifiers:
  Comparative and
  Superlative

Vocabulary
■ Figurative Language

```
┌─────────────────────────────────────────┐
│            MISSOURI PLANNER               │
│        Grade-Level Expectations           │
│  R1.C, R1.D, R1.F, R1.G, R1.H, R1.I, R2.A, R2.B, │
│  R2.C, W1.A, IL1.A, IL1.B, IL1.C          │
└─────────────────────────────────────────┘
```

Preparing to Read
____ Connect to Your Life
____ Build Background
____ Focus Your Reading
     Literary Analysis: Sonnet   ❑ Unit Six Resource Book: Literary Analysis SkillBuilder, p. 9
     Active Reading: Determining Major Ideas in   ❑ Unit Six Resource Book: Active Reading SkillBuilder, p. 8
     a Poem

Teaching the Literature
____ Reading the Selection   ❑ PE pp. 940–944

Thinking Through the Literature
____ Connect to the Literature
____ Think Critically   ❑ Reading and Critical Thinking Transparencies, T12, T48
____ Extend Interpretations
____ Literary Analysis: Sonnet   ❑ Literary Analysis Transparencies, T11

Choices and Challenges

Writing Options
____ Slogan About New York
____ Write a Review

Inquiry and Research
____ Art

Teaching Options (from Teacher's Edition)

Mini Lessons

Vocabulary Strategy
____ Figurative Language   ❑ Vocabulary Transparencies and Copymasters, C77

Grammar
____ Modifiers: Comparative and Superlative   ❑ Grammar Transparencies and Copymasters, C132

Speaking and Listening
____ Reading Poetry

Assessment
____ Selection Test   ❑ Formal Assessment: Selection Test, pp. 171–172
____ Test Generator

Homework Assignments	Other Teaching Materials
_____	_____
_____	_____
_____	_____
_____	_____
_____	_____

If We Must Die / A Black Man Talks of Reaping   Pages 945–949

Core Objectives
- Understand and appreciate two poems
- Identify and examine extended metaphor
- Distinguish figurative and literal meaning

<table>
<tr><td colspan="2" align="center">MISSOURI PLANNER
Grade-Level Expectations</td></tr>
<tr><td colspan="2">R1.C, R1.D, R1.F, R1.G, R1.H, R1.I, R2.A, R2.B,
R2.C, W1.A, W3.C</td></tr>
</table>

Integrating Skills

Grammar	Vocabulary
■ Modifiers	■ Prefixes

Preparing to Read
___ Connect to Your Life
___ Build Background
___ Focus Your Reading
     Literary Analysis: Extended Metaphor   ❑ Unit Six Resource Book: Literary Analysis SkillBuilder, p. 11
     Active Reading: Distinguishing Figurative and   ❑ Unit Six Resource Book: Active Reading SkillBuilder, p. 10
        Literal Meaning

Teaching the Literature
___ Reading the Selection   ❑ PE pp. 945–949

Thinking Through the Literature
___ Connect to the Literature
___ Think Critically   ❑ Reading and Critical Thinking Transparencies, T23, T56
___ Extend Interpretations
___ Literary Analysis: Extended Metaphor

Choices and Challenges
Writing Options
___ Problem-Solution Essay
___ Write a Sonnet

Activities and Explorations
___ Activist Poster

If We Must Die / A Black Man Talks of Reaping

Teaching Options (from Teacher's Edition)

Mini Lessons

Vocabulary Strategy

____ Prefixes *In-* and *Out-*   ❏ Vocabulary Transparencies and Copymasters, C78

Grammar

____ Modifiers: Use of *-er*   ❏ Grammar Transparencies and Copymasters, C135

____ *Informal Assessment*

Assessment

____ Selection Test   ❏ Formal Assessment: Selection Test, pp. 173–174

____ Test Generator

Homework Assignments

_____

_____

_____

_____

_____

Other Teaching Materials

_____

_____

_____

_____

How It Feels to Be Colored Me

Core Objectives
- Understand and appreciate an autobiographical essay
- Draw conclusions about author's purpose

MISSOURI PLANNER
Grade-Level Expectations
R1.C, R1.D, R1.F, R1.G, R1.H, R1.I, R2.A, R2.C, W1.A

Integrating Skills
Grammar	Vocabulary
- Modifiers: Distinguishing *Those* from *Them*	- Using Context Clues - Using Context Clues with Figurative Language

Preparing to Read
____ Connect to Your Life
____ Build Background
____ Vocabulary Preview: Using Context Clues   ❑ Unit Six Resource Book: Words to Know SkillBuilder, p. 15
____ Focus Your Reading
    Literary Analysis: Autobiographical Essay   ❑ Unit Six Resource Book: Literary Analysis SkillBuilder, p. 14
    Active Reading: Drawing Conclusions About   ❑ Unit Six Resource Book: Active Reading SkillBuilder, p. 13
       Author's Purposes

Teaching the Literature
                                         ❑ PE pp. 950–958
____ Reading the Selection   ❑ Unit Six Resource Book: Summary, p. 12

Thinking Through the Literature
____ Connect to the Literature
____ Think Critically   ❑ Reading and Critical Thinking Transparencies, T4, T19
____ Extend Interpretations
____ Literary Analysis: Autobiographical Essay   ❑ Literary Analysis Transparencies, T20

Choices and Challenges
Writing Options
____ Proposal for School Assembly
____ Autobiographical Essay

Vocabulary in Action
____ Meaning Clues

____ **Author Activity**

How It Feels to Be Colored Me

Teaching Options (from Teacher's Edition)

Mini Lessons

Preteaching Vocabulary
____ Using Context Clues

Vocabulary Strategy
____ Using Context Clues with Figurative Language

❑ Vocabulary Transparencies and Copymasters, C79

Grammar
____ Modifiers: Distinguishing *Those* from *Them*

❑ Grammar Transparencies and Copymasters, C138

Viewing and Representing
Art Appreciation
____ *Skipping Along* by Stephen Scott Young
____ *Bal Jeunesse* by Palmer Hayden

Informal Assessment
____ Writing Letters to the Author

Assessment
____ Selection Quiz
____ Selection Test
____ Test Generator

❑ Unit Six Resource Book: Selection Quiz, p. 16
❑ Formal Assessment: Selection Test, pp. 175–176

Homework Assignments

_____

_____

_____

_____

_____

Other Teaching Materials

_____

_____

_____

_____

_____

My Dungeon Shook

Core Objectives
- Understand and appreciate an open letter
- Analyze characteristics of clearly written texts

Integrating Skills

Grammar
- Parallel Compound Predicates

Vocabulary
- Using Context to Determine Connotations
- Denotation and Connotation

> **MISSOURI PLANNER**
> Grade-Level Expectations
> R1.C, R1.D, R1.E, R1.F, R1.G, R1.H, R1.I, R2.A, R2.C, W1.A, W3.C, IL1.A, IL1.B, IL1.C

Preparing to Read
____ Comparing Literature
____ Build Background
____ Vocabulary Preview: Using Context to Determine Connotations   ❑ Unit Six Resource Book: Words to Know SkillBuilder, p. 20
____ Focus Your Reading
      Literary Analysis: Open Letter   ❑ Unit Six Resource Book: Literary Analysis SkillBuilder, p. 19
      Active Reading: Analyzing Characteristics of   ❑ Unit Six Resource Book: Active Reading SkillBuilder, p. 18
      Clearly Written Texts

Teaching the Literature
     ❑ PE pp. 959–966
____ Reading the Selection   ❑ Unit One Resource Book: Summary, p.17

Thinking Through the Literature
____ Connect to the Literature
____ Think Critically   ❑ Reading and Critical Thinking Transparencies, T15
____ Extend Interpretations
____ Literary Analysis: Open Letter   ❑ Literary Analysis Transparencies, T23

Choices and Challenges

Writing Options
____ Points of Comparison
____ Personal Response
____ Compare-Contrast Essay

Activities and Explorations
____ Commencement Address
____ Photo Gallery of Harlem
____ Group Discussion

Inquiry and Research
____ Music

Vocabulary in Action
____ Context Clues

My Dungeon Shook

Teaching Options (from Teacher's Edition)

Mini Lessons

Preteaching Vocabulary
____ Using Context to Determine Connotation

Vocabulary Strategy
____ Denotation and Connotation   ❑ Vocabulary Transparencies and Copymasters, C80

Grammar
____ Parallel Compound Predicates   ❑ Grammar Transparencies and Copymasters, C165, T57

Viewing and Representing
Art Appreciation
____ *My Brother* by John Wilson

Informal Assessment
____ Making Inferences and Generalizations

Assessment
____ Selection Quiz   ❑ Unit Six Resource Book: Selection Quiz, p. 21
____ Selection Test   ❑ Formal Assessment: Selection Test, pp. 177–178
____ Test Generator

Homework Assignments
_____
_____
_____
_____
_____

Other Teaching Materials
_____
_____
_____
_____
_____

Life for My Child Is Simple / Primer for Blacks   Pages 967–972

Core Objectives
- Understand and appreciate two poems
- Identify and examine style in poetry
- Compare and contrast poems

```
┌─────────────────────────────────────┐
│           MISSOURI PLANNER           │
│      Grade-Level Expectations        │
│ R1.C, R1.D, R1.F, R1.G, R1.H, R1.I, R2.A, R2.C, │
│ W1.A                                 │
└─────────────────────────────────────┘
```

Integrating Skills

Grammar
- Parallel Series

Vocabulary
- Prefixes

Preparing to Read
____ Comparing Literature
____ Build Background
____ Focus Your Reading
    Literary Analysis: Style
    Active Reading: Comparing and Contrasting
    Poems

❑ Unit Six Resource Book: Literary Analysis SkillBuilder, p. 23
❑ Unit Six Resource Book: Active Reading SkillBuilder, p. 22

Teaching the Literature
____ Reading the Selection

❑ PE pp. 967–972

Thinking Through the Literature
____ Connect to the Literature
____ Think Critically
____ Extend Interpretations
____ Literary Analysis: Style

❑ Reading and Critical Thinking Transparencies, T15, T41

Choices and Challenges
Writing Options
____ Points of Comparison
____ Yearbook Biography
____ Summary of Brooks's Message

Activities and Explorations
____ T-shirt Emblem
____ Preach a Sermon

____ **Author Activity**

Life for My Child Is Simple / Primer for Blacks

Teaching Options (from Teacher's Edition)

Mini Lessons

Vocabulary Strategy

____ Prefixes

❑ Vocabulary Transparencies and Copymasters, C81

Grammar

____ Parallel Series

❑ Grammar Transparencies and Copymasters, C166, T54, T57

Speaking and Listening

____ Roundtable Discussion

Informal Assessment

____ Predicting Probable Outcomes

Assessment

____ Selection Test

____ Test Generator

❑ Formal Assessment: Selection Test, pp. 179–180

Homework Assignments

_____

_____

_____

_____

_____

Other Teaching Materials

_____

_____

_____

_____

_____

Thoughts on the African-American Novel

Pages 973–977

Core Objectives
- Understand and appreciate an essay of literary criticism
- Identify major ideas in an essay

Integrating Skills

Grammar
- Varying Sentence Beginnings

Vocabulary
- Greek and Latin Roots

> **MISSOURI PLANNER**
> Grade-Level Expectations
> R1.C, R1.D, R1.F, R1.G, R1.H, R1.I, R2.A, R2.C, W1.A, IL1.A, IL1.B, IL1.C

Preparing to Read
____ Comparing Literature
____ Build Background
____ Focus Your Reading
     Literary Analysis: Literary Criticism   ❑ Unit Six Resource Book: Literary Analysis SkillBuilder, p. 26
     Active Reading: Identifying Major Ideas   ❑ Unit Six Resource Book: Active Reading SkillBuilder, p. 25

Teaching the Literature
____ Reading the Selection

❑ PE pp. 973–977
❑ Unit Six Resource Book: Summary, p. 24

Thinking Through the Literature
____ Connect to the Literature
____ Think Critically   ❑ Reading and Critical Thinking Transparencies, T12, T51, T60
____ Extend Interpretations
____ Literary Analysis: Literary Criticism

Choices and Challenges

Writing Options
____ Letter to Toni Morrison
____ Points of Comparison
____ Essay About Art Form

Activities and Explorations
____ Illustration

Inquiry and Research
____ Origin of the Novel

Author Activity

Thoughts on the African-American Novel

Teaching Options (from Teacher's Edition)

Mini Lessons

Vocabulary Strategy
____ Greek and Latin Roots

❑ Vocabulary Transparencies and Copymasters, C82

Grammar
____ Varying Sentence Beginnings

❑ Grammar Transparencies and Copymasters, C167

Informal Assessment
____ Using a Chorus

Assessment

____ Selection Quiz

____ Selection Test

____ Part Test

____ Test Generator

❑ Unit Six Resource Book: Selection Quiz, p. 27

❑ Formal Assessment: Selection Test, p. 181

❑ Formal Assessment: Unit Six, Part 1 Test, pp. 183–184

Homework Assignments

_____

_____

_____

_____

_____

Other Teaching Materials

_____

_____

_____

_____

_____

Research Report

Writing Prompt
Write a historical research report about some aspect
of the Harlem Renaissance or another topic that
your teacher approves.

> **MISSOURI PLANNER**
> Grade-Level Expectations
> R3.D, W1.A, W2.C, W2.D, W2.E, W2.F, W3.B,
> W3.C, W3.D, IL1.A, IL1.B, IL1.C, IL.1.D

Preparing to Read

____ Introduction
____ Basics in a Box
____ Using the Graphic

❏ Writing Transparencies and Copymasters, T11, T20, C33

____ Analyzing a Student Model
"Zora Neale Hurston"

❏ Unit Six Resource Book: Student Models, pp. 34–39

Writing

____ **Prewriting and Exploring**
Choosing a Subject
Planning the Research Report
Researching

❏ Unit Six Resource Book: Prewriting, p. 29

____ **Drafting**
Organizing the Draft

❏ Unit Six Resource Book: Drafting and Elaboration, p. 30

____ **Peer Review**
Ask Your Peer Reader

❏ Unit Six Resource Book: Peer Response Guide, pp. 31–32

____ **Revising**
Elaborating—Details and Examples

❏ Unit Six Resource Book: Revising, Editing, and Proofreading, p. 33
❏ Unit Six Resource Book: Rubric for Evaluation, p. 40

____ **Editing and Proofreading**
Using Commas

____ **Reflecting**

Homework Assignments

_____
_____
_____
_____
_____

Other Teaching Materials

_____
_____
_____
_____
_____

Selected Poems by Robert Frost

Core Objectives
- Understand and appreciate classic poetry
- Identify and examine mood in poetry
- Analyze word choice

> **MISSOURI PLANNER**
> Grade-Level Expectations
> R1.C, R1.D, R1.F, R1.G, R1.H, R1.I, R2.A, R2.C

Integrating Skills

Grammar
- Adjective Elements

Vocabulary
- Connotation and Denotation

Preparing to Read
____ Connect to Your Life
____ Build Background
____ Focus Your Reading
     Literary Analysis: Mood in Poetry   ❑ Unit Six Resource Book: Literary Analysis SkillBuilder, p. 44
     Active Reading: Analyzing Word Choice   ❑ Unit Six Resource Book: Active Reading SkillBuilder, p. 43

Teaching the Literature
____ Reading the Selection   ❑ PE pp. 1000–1005

Thinking Through the Literature
____ Connect to the Literature
____ Think Critically   ❑ Reading and Critical Thinking Transparencies, T50
____ Extend Interpretations
____ Literary Analysis: Mood   ❑ Literary Analysis Transparencies, T18

Teaching Options (from Teacher's Edition)

Mini Lessons

Vocabulary Strategy
____ Discriminate Between Connotation and   ❑ Vocabulary Transparencies and Copymasters, C83
     Denotation

Grammar
____ Adjective Elements   ❑ Grammar Transparencies and Copymasters, C141

Cross Curricular Link

History
____ The Berlin Wall

Informal Assessment
____ Make Inferences and Draw Conclusions

Selected Poems by Robert Frost

Assessment

____ Selection Test

____ Test Generator

❑ Formal Assessment: Selection Test, pp. 185–186

Homework Assignments

_____

_____

_____

_____

_____

Other Teaching Materials

_____

_____

_____

_____

_____

The Death of the Hired Man

Core Objectives
- Understand and appreciate a narrative poem
- Examine blank verse
- Understand form in poetry

MISSOURI PLANNER

Grade-Level Expectations

R1.C, R1.D, R1.F, R1.G, R1.H, R1.I, R2.A, R2.C, W1.A, IL1.A, IL1.B, IL1.C

Integrating Skills

Grammar
- Modifiers

Vocabulary
- Using Context Clues
- Connotation

Preparing to Read
____ Connect to Your Life
____ Build Background
____ Vocabulary Preview: Using Context Clues: ❏ Unit Six Resource Book: Words to Know SkillBuilder, p. 48
Summary Statements
____ Focus Your Reading
Literary Analysis: Blank Verse   ❏ Unit Six Resource Book: Literary Analysis SkillBuilder, p. 47
Active Reading: Understanding Form in Poetry   ❏ Unit Six Resource Book: Active Reading SkillBuilder, p. 46

Teaching the Literature
                                                    ❏ PE pp. 1006–1015
____ Reading the Selection   ❏ Unit Six Resource Book: Summary, p. 45

Thinking Through the Literature
____ Connect to the Literature
____ Think Critically   ❏ Reading and Critical Thinking Transparencies, T26
____ Extend Interpretations
____ Literary Analysis: Blank Verse   ❏ Literary Analysis Transparencies, T12

Choices and Challenges

Writing Options
____ Neighborly Editorial

Activities and Explorations
____ New England Collage

Inquiry and Research
____ Farm Life

Vocabulary in Action
____ Synonyms

Author Study Presentation
____ Living Museum Project

The Death of the Hired Man

Teaching Options (from Teacher's Edition)

Mini Lessons

Preteaching Vocabulary
____ Using Context Clues: Summary Statements

Vocabulary Strategy
____ Interpret the Connotative Power of Words   ❏ Vocabulary Transparencies and Copymasters, C84

Grammar
____ Problems with Modifiers: *This, These, That,*   ❏ Grammar Transparencies and Copymasters, C139
Those

Cross Curricular Link

Workplace
____ Communicating Ideas

Informal Assessment
____ Journal Entries

Assessment

____ Selection Quiz   ❏ Unit Six Resource Book: Selection Quiz, p. 49
____ Selection Test   ❏ Formal Assessment: Selection Test, pp. 187–188
____ Test Generator

Homework Assignments

_____

_____

_____

_____

_____

Other Teaching Materials

_____

_____

_____

_____

_____

The End of Something

Core Objectives
- Understand a modernist short story
- Identify and examine style
- Make inferences in a short story

> **MISSOURI PLANNER**
> Grade-Level Expectations
> R1.C, R1.D, R1.F, R1.G, R1.H, R1.I, R2.A, R2.C, W1.A

Integrating Skills

Grammar
- Modifiers: Illogical Comparisons
- Commas with Direct Quotations

Vocabulary
- Relying on Context to Determine Connotation

Preparing to Read
___ Connect to Your Life
___ Build Background
___ Focus Your Reading
     Literary Analysis: Style   ❑ Unit Six Resource Book: Literary Analysis SkillBuilder, p. 52
     Active Reading: Making Inferences   ❑ Unit Six Resource Book: Active Reading SkillBuilder, p. 51

Teaching the Literature
       ❑ PE pp. 1018–1024
___ Reading the Selection   ❑ Unit Six Resource Book: Summary, p. 50

Thinking Through the Literature
___ Connect to the Literature
___ Think Critically   ❑ Reading and Critical Thinking Transparencies, T7
___ Extend Interpretations
___ Literary Analysis: Style   ❑ Literary Analysis Transparencies, T17

Choices and Challenges
Writing Options
___ Personal Ad
___ Advice Letters
___ TV Script

Activities and Explorations
___ Story Illustrations
___ Survey of Romantic Breakups

The End of Something

Teaching Options (from Teacher's Edition)

Mini Lessons

Vocabulary Strategy

____ Relying on Context to Determine Connotations of Words

❏ Vocabulary Transparencies and Copymasters, C85

Grammar

____ Modifiers: Illogical Comparisons

❏ Grammar Transparencies and Copymasters, C134

____ Commas: Setting Off Quotations

❏ Grammar Transparencies and Copymasters, C154, T56

Viewing and Representing

Art Appreciation

____ *Canoe* by David Park

Informal Assessment

____ Story Map

Assessment

____ Selection Quiz

❏ Unit Six Resource Book: Selection Quiz, p. 53

____ Selection Test

❏ Formal Assessment: Selection Test, pp. 189–190

____ Test Generator

Homework Assignments

_____

_____

_____

_____

_____

Other Teaching Materials

_____

_____

_____

_____

_____

The Love Song of J. Alfred Prufrock   **Pages 1025–1032**

Core Objectives
- Understand and appreciate a classic modernist poem
- Identify and appreciate imagery
- Understand stream of consciousness

MISSOURI PLANNER

Grade-Level Expectations

R1.C, R1.D, R1.F, R1.G, R1.H, R1.I, R2.A, R2.C, W1.A, IL1.A, IL1.B, IL1.C

Integrating Skills

Grammar
- Inverted Subjects and Verbs

Vocabulary
- Context Clues
- Understanding Figurative Language Through Context

Preparing to Read
____ Connect to Your Life
____ Build Background
____ Vocabulary Preview: Context Clues   ❑ Unit Six Resource Book: Words to Know SkillBuilder, p. 57
____ Focus Your Reading
     Literary Analysis: Imagery   ❑ Unit Six Resource Book: Literary Analysis SkillBuilder, p. 56
     Active Reading: Understanding Stream of   ❑ Unit Six Resource Book: Active Reading SkillBuilder, p. 55
     Consciousness

Teaching the Literature
____ Reading the Selection   ❑ PE pp. 1025–1032
                               ❑ Unit Six Resource Book: Summary, p. 54

Thinking Through the Literature
____ Connect to the Literature
____ Think Critically   ❑ Reading and Critical Thinking Transparencies, T9
____ Extend Interpretations
____ Literary Analysis: Imagery   ❑ Literary Analysis Transparencies, T17

Choices and Challenges
Writing Options
____ Letter to Prufrock
____ Partygoers Narrative
____ Social Commentary

Activities and Explorations
____ Improvisational Scene
____ Prufrock's Caricature
____ Radio Talk Show

Inquiry and Research
____ Michelangelo's Artistic Genius

Vocabulary in Action
____ Synonyms
____ Exercise B

The Love Song of J. Alfred Prufrock

Choices and Challenges (continued)

Author Activity
____ Broadway Smash Hit

Teaching Options (from Teacher's Edition)

Mini Lessons

Preteaching Vocabulary
____ Context Clues   ❏ Vocabulary Transparencies and Copymasters, C86

Vocabulary Strategy
____ Understanding Figurative Language Through Context

Grammar
____ Inverted Subjects and Verbs   ❏ Grammar Transparencies and Copymasters, C78

Cross Curricular Link

Humanities
____ Modernism

Informal Assessment
____ Making Inferences and Drawing Conclusions

Assessment
____ Selection Quiz   ❏ Unit Six Resource Book: Selection Quiz, p. 58
____ Selection Test   ❏ Formal Assessment: Selection Test, pp. 191–192
____ Test Generator

Homework Assignments	Other Teaching Materials
_____	_____
_____	_____
_____	_____
_____	_____
_____	_____

The Jilting of Granny Weatherall

Core Objectives
- Understand and appreciate a modernist short story
- Understand a stream-of-consciousness narrative
- Use sequencing to untangle events

Integrating Skills

Grammar	Vocabulary
■ Parallel Compound Subjects	■ Using Context Clues
■ Colon	■ Figurative Language and Idioms

```
┌──────────────────────────────────────────┐
│            MISSOURI PLANNER                │
│         Grade-Level Expectations           │
│  R1.C, R1.D, R1.F, R1.G, R1.H, R1.I, R2.A, R2.C, │
│  W1.A                                      │
└──────────────────────────────────────────┘
```

Preparing to Read
____ Connect to Your Life
____ Build Background
____ Vocabulary Preview: Context Clues   ❏ Unit Six Resource Book: Words to Know SkillBuilder, p. 62
____ Focus Your Reading
     Literary Analysis: Stream of Consciousness   ❏ Unit Six Resource Book: Literary Analysis SkillBuilder, p. 61
     Active Reading: Sequencing   ❏ Unit Six Resource Book: Active Reading SkillBuilder, p. 60

Teaching the Literature
____ Reading the Selection   ❏ PE pp. 1034–1044
     ❏ Unit Six Resource Book: Summary, p. 59

Thinking Through the Literature
____ Connect to the Literature
____ Think Critically
____ Extend Interpretations
____ Literary Analysis: Stream of Consciousness   ❏ Literary Analysis Transparencies, T17

Choices and Challenges
Writing Options
____ Eulogy for Granny
____ Psychological Profile

Activities and Explorations
____ Story Illustration
____ Tabloid Interview

Vocabulary in Action
____ Analogies

The Jilting of Granny Weatherall

Teaching Options (from Teacher's Edition)

Mini Lessons

Preteaching Vocabulary
____ Context Clues

Vocabulary Strategy
____ Using Context Clues for Figurative
Language and Idioms

❑ Vocabulary Transparencies and Copymasters, C87

Grammar
____ Parallel Compound Subjects
____ Colon as a Sentence Connector

❑ Grammar Transparencies and Copymasters, C168
❑ Grammar Transparencies and Copymasters, C159, T57

Viewing and Representing
Art Appreciation
____ *Portrait of Ambroise Vollard* by Pablo Picasso
____ *Yvonne and Magdaleine Torn in Tatters*
by Marcel Duchamp

Cross Curricular Link

Women's Studies
____ Role of Antebellum Southern Women

Informal Assessment
____ Understanding Character

Assessment

____ Selection Quiz
____ Selection Test
____ Test Generator

❑ Unit Six Resource Book: Selection Quiz, p. 63
❑ Formal Assessment: Selection Test, pp. 193–194

Homework Assignments

_____
_____
_____
_____
_____

Other Teaching Materials

_____
_____
_____
_____
_____

The Man Who Was Almost a Man

Core Objectives
- Understand and appreciate a short story
- Understand point of view
- Make judgments about the main character's decisions

```
                                    MISSOURI PLANNER
                                  Grade-Level Expectations
                              R1.C, R1.D, R1.F, R1.G, R1.H, R1.I, R2.A, R2.C,
                              W1.A, IL.2.A
```

Integrating Skills

Grammar
- Creating Complex Sentences
- Quotation Marks with Other Punctuation

Vocabulary
- Dictionaries and Slang

Preparing to Read
____ Connect to Your Life
____ Build Background
____ Focus Your Reading
    Literary Analysis: Point of View   ❑ Unit Six Resource Book: Literary Analysis SkillBuilder, p. 66
    Active Reading: Making Judgments   ❑ Unit Six Resource Book: Active Reading SkillBuilder, p. 65

Teaching the Literature
____ Reading the Selection   ❑ PE pp. 1045–1056
                                       ❑ Unit Six Resource Book: Summary, p. 64

Thinking Through the Literature
____ Connect to the Literature
____ Think Critically   ❑ Reading and Critical Thinking Transparencies, T5
____ Extend Interpretations
____ Literary Analysis: Point of View   ❑ Literary Analysis Transparencies, T20

Choices and Challenges

Writing Options
____ Defining Adulthood
____ Letter Home
____ Editorial

Activities and Explorations
____ Dramatic Reading
____ Charting Expenses
____ Film Critics' Circle

Author Activity
____ The Creation of Characters

The Man Who Was Almost a Man

Teaching Options (from Teacher's Edition)

Mini Lessons

Vocabulary Strategy
____ Dictionaries and Slang

❏ Vocabulary Transparencies and Copymasters, C88

Grammar
____ Creating Complex Sentences
____ Quotation Marks with Other Punctuation

❏ Grammar Transparencies and Copymasters, C169
❏ Grammar Transparencies and Copymasters, C162, T56

Speaking and Listening
____ Pronunciation of Dialect

Viewing and Representing
____ Photographs

Cross Curricular Links

U.S. History
____ 1910

Economics
____ African-American Sharecroppers in the Early 20th Century

Workplace
____ Writing an Evaluation

Informal Assessment
____ Predicting What Happens Next

Assessment
____ Selection Quiz
____ Selection Test
____ Test Generator

❏ Unit Six Resource Book: Selection Quiz, p. 67
❏ Formal Assessment: Selection Test, pp. 195–196

Homework Assignments
_____
_____
_____
_____
_____

Other Teaching Materials
_____
_____
_____
_____
_____

Mirror / Self in 1958

Core Objectives
- Understand and appreciate two confessional poems
- Identify and examine the speaker in poetry
- Link title and theme

MISSOURI PLANNER

Grade-Level Expectations

R1.C, R1.D, R1.F, R1.G, R1.H, R1.I, R2.A, R2.C, W1.A, W3.C

Integrating Skills

Grammar
- Compound Sentences
- Capitalizing Family Titles

Vocabulary
- Word Origins: Mirror

Preparing to Read

____ Comparing Literature
____ Build Background
____ Focus Your Reading
    Literary Analysis: Speaker   ❑   Unit Six Resource Book: Literary Analysis SkillBuilder, p. 69
    Active Reading: Linking Title and Theme   ❑   Unit Six Resource Book: Active Reading SkillBuilder, p. 68

Teaching the Literature

____ Reading the Selection   ❑   PE pp. 1057–1063

Thinking Through the Literature

____ Connect to the Literature
____ Think Critically   ❑   Reading and Critical Thinking Transparencies, T48
____ Extend Interpretations
____ Literary Analysis: Speaker   ❑   Literary Analysis Transparencies, T23

Choices and Challenges

Writing Options
____ Diary of a Housewife
____ Poetic Riddle
____ Points of Comparison

Activities and Explorations
____ Face-to-Face Conversation
____ A Doll's House

Inquiry and Research
____ Women's Roles
____ Confessional Poets

Mirror / Self in 1958

Teaching Options (from Teacher's Edition)

Mini Lessons

Vocabulary Strategy

____ Researching Word Origins: Mirror ❑ Vocabulary Transparencies and Copymasters, C89

Grammar

____ Creating Compound Sentences ❑ Grammar Transparencies and Copymasters, C170

____ Capitalizing Family Titles ❑ Grammar Transparencies and Copymasters, C143

Informal Assessment

____ Making Inferences

Assessment

____ Selection Test ❑ Formal Assessment: Selection Test, pp. 197–198

____ Part Test ❑ Formal Assessment: Unit Six, Part 2, pp. 199–200

____ Test Generator

Homework Assignments

_____

_____

_____

_____

_____

Other Teaching Materials

_____

_____

_____

_____

_____

Armistice

Core Objectives
- Understand and appreciate a short story
- Explore connections between theme and title
- Draw conclusions about character motivation

> **MISSOURI PLANNER**
> Grade-Level Expectations
> R1.C, R1.D, R1.E, R1.F, R1.G, R1.H, R1.I, R2.A, R2.C, W1.A, IL1.A, IL1.B, IL1.C

Integrating Skills

Grammar
- Complements

Vocabulary
- Using Context Clues
- Applying Meanings of Prefixes

Preparing to Read
____ Connect to Your Life
____ Build Background
____ Vocabulary Preview: Using Context Clues   ❏ Unit Seven Resource Book: Words to Know SkillBuilder, p. 7
____ Focus Your Reading
         Literary Analysis: Theme and Title   ❏ Unit Seven Resource Book: Literary Analysis SkillBuilder, p. 6
         Active Reading: Drawing Conclusions About   ❏ Unit Seven Resource Book: Active Reading SkillBuilder, p. 5
         Character Motivation

Teaching the Literature
                                                       ❏ PE pp. 1076–1087
____ Reading the Selection   ❏ Unit Seven Resource Book: Summary, p. 4

Thinking Through the Literature
____ Connect to the Literature
____ Think Critically   ❏ Reading and Critical Thinking Transparencies, T4
____ Extend Interpretations
____ Literary Analysis: Theme and Title   ❏ Literary Analysis Transparencies, T20

Choices and Challenges

Writing Options
____ Dream Analysis
____ Letter to the Editor
____ Eventful Paragraph
____ World War II Presentation

Activities and Explorations
____ Readers Theater Performance
____ Memory Illustration

Inquiry and Research
____ History of Anti-Semitism
____ German Victory

Art Connection
____ Conflicting Impression

Armistice

Choices and Challenges (continued)

Vocabulary in Action
____ Context Clues

Author Activity
____ Grave Pronouncement

Teaching Options (from Teacher's Edition)

Mini Lessons

Preteaching Vocabulary
____ Using Context Clues

Vocabulary Strategy
____ Applying Meanings of Prefixes   ❑ Vocabulary Transparencies and Copymasters, C90

Grammar
____ Complements   ❑ Grammar Transparencies and Copymasters, C79

Speaking and Listening
____ Role Playing

Viewing and Representing
Art Appreciation
____ *What Will Become of Us?* by George Skirigin
____ Photograph

Cross Curricular Link

History
____ Summary of Major Events of World War II

Informal Assessment
____ Understanding Character and Style

Assessment

____ Selection Quiz   ❑ Unit Seven Resource Book: Selection Quiz, p. 8
____ Selection Test   ❑ Formal Assessment: Selection Test, pp. 201–202
____ Test Generator

Homework Assignments

_____
_____
_____
_____
_____

Other Teaching Materials

_____
_____
_____
_____
_____

The Death of the Ball Turret Gunner /
Why Soldiers Won't Talk

Core Objectives
- Understand and appreciate a poem and an essay
- Understand how imagery conveys tone
- Adjust reading strategies for different genres

```
                                         MISSOURI PLANNER
                                      Grade-Level Expectations
                                 R1.C, R1.D, R1.F, R1.G, R1.H, R1.I, R2.A, R2.C,
                                 W1.A, IL1.A, IL1.B, IL1.C
```

Integrating Skills
Grammar
- Rhythm vs. Redundancy

Vocabulary
- Suffixes

Preparing to Read
____ Connect to Your Life
____ Build Background
____ Focus Your Reading:
Literary Analysis: Imagery and Tone ❑ Unit Seven Resource Book: Literary Analysis SkillBuilder, p. 11
Active Reading: Adjusting Reading Strategies ❑ Unit Seven Resource Book: Active Reading SkillBuilder, p. 10

Teaching the Literature
❑ PE pp. 1088–1094
____ Reading the Selection ❑ Unit Seven Resource Book: Summary, p. 9

Thinking Through the Literature
____ Connect to the Literature
____ Think Critically ❑ Reading and Critical Thinking Transparencies, T8, T12, T39
____ Extend Interpretations
____ Literary Analysis: Imagery and Tone

Choices and Challenges
Writing Options
____ Grave Inscriptions
____ Personal Narrative

Activities and Explorations
____ Interview with a Veteran
____ Model Plane

Inquiry and Research
____ Shell Shock

The Death of the Ball Turret Gunner / Why Soldiers Won't Talk

Teaching Options (from Teacher's Edition)

Mini Lessons

Vocabulary Strategy

____ Suffixes

❏ Vocabulary Transparencies and Copymasters, C91

Grammar

____ Rhythm: Repetition vs. Redundancy

❏ Grammar Transparencies and Copymasters, C171

Speaking and Listening

____ Interview

Informal Assessment

____ Write a Letter

Assessment

____ Selection Quiz

❏ Unit Seven Resource Book: Selection Quiz, p. 12

____ Selection Test

❏ Formal Assessment: Selection Test, pp. 203–204

____ Test Generator

Homework Assignments

_____

_____

_____

_____

_____

Other Teaching Materials

_____

_____

_____

_____

_____

Letter from Paradise /
In Response to Executive Order 9066

Core Objectives
- Understand and appreciate an essay and a poem
- Understand mood
- Compare mood in an essay and a poem

MISSOURI PLANNER
Grade-Level Expectations
R1.C, R1.D, R1.F, R1.G, R1.H, R1.I, R2.A, R2.B, R2.C, W1.A, IL1.A, IL1.B, IL1.C

Integrating Skills
Grammar
- The Placement of *Only*

Vocabulary
- Prefixes

Preparing to Read
___ Connect to Your Life
___ Build Background
___ Focus Your Reading
    Literary Analysis: Mood   ❑ Unit Seven Resource Book: Literary Analysis SkillBuilder, p. 15
    Active Reading: Comparing Mood   ❑ Unit Seven Resource Book: Active Reading SkillBuilder, p. 14

Teaching the Literature
                                     ❑ PE pp. 1095–1102
___ Reading the Selection   ❑ Unit Seven Resource Book: Summary, p. 13

Thinking Through the Literature
___ Connect to the Literature
___ Think Critically   ❑ Reading and Critical Thinking Transparencies, T15
___ Extend Interpretations
___ Literary Analysis: Mood   ❑ Literary Analysis Transparencies, T20

Choices and Challenges
Writing Options
___ Family Memoir

Activities and Explorations
___ Contrasting Cartoons

Inquiry and Research
___ Japanese-American Internment

Letter from Paradise /
In Response to Executive Order 9066

Teaching Options (from Teacher's Edition)

Mini Lessons

Vocabulary Strategy
____ Prefixes

❏ Vocabulary Transparencies and Copymasters, C90

Grammar
____ The Placement of *Only*

Speaking and Listening
____ Poem Recitation

Cross Curricular Link

History
____ Pearl Harbor

Informal Assessment
____ Understanding Mood

Assessment

____ Selection Quiz
____ Selection Test
____ Test Generator

❏ Unit Seven Resource Book: Selection Quiz, p. 16
❏ Formal Assessment: Selection Test, pp. 205–206

Homework Assignments

_____
_____
_____
_____
_____

Other Teaching Materials

_____
_____
_____
_____
_____

Ambush

Core Objectives
- Understand and appreciate a short story
- Understand internal conflict
- Connect the story to personal experience

MISSOURI PLANNER
Grade-Level Expectations
R1.C, R1.D, R1.F, R1.G, R1.H, R1.I, R2.A, R2.C,
W1.A, W3.C, IL1.A, IL1.B, IL1.C

Integrating Skills

Grammar	Vocabulary
■ Adverbs: Qualifiers	■ Context Clues

Preparing to Read
___ Comparing Literature
___ Build Background
___ Focus Your Reading:
   Literary Analysis: Internal Conflict   ❏ Unit Seven Resource Book: Literary Analysis SkillBuilder, p. 19
   Active Reading: Connecting to Experience   ❏ Unit Seven Resource Book: Active Reading SkillBuilder, p. 18

Teaching the Literature
                                                 ❏ PE pp. 1105–1110
___ Reading the Selection   ❏ Unit Seven Resource Book: Summary, p. 17

Thinking Through the Literature
___ Connect to the Literature
___ Think Critically   ❏ Reading and Critical Thinking Transparencies, T9, T58
___ Extend Interpretations
___ Literary Analysis: Internal Conflict   ❏ Literary Analysis Transparencies, T15

Choices and Challenges
Writing Options
___ Exhibit Proposal
___ Points of Comparison

Activities and Explorations
___ Movie Score

Inquiry and Research
___ Guerrilla Tactics

Author Activity
___ Real-Life Experience

Ambush

....

Teaching Options (from Teacher's Edition)

Mini Lessons

Vocabulary Strategy

____ Context Clues   ❑   Vocabulary Transparencies and Copymasters, C92

Grammar

____ Adverbs: Qualifiers   ❑   Grammar Transparencies and Copymasters, C71

Viewing and Representing

Art Appreciation

____ *Fenixes* by Rupert Garcia

Assessment

____ Selection Quiz   ❑   Unit Seven Resource Book: Selection Quiz, p. 20

____ Selection Test   ❑   Formal Assessment: Selection Test, pp. 207–208

____ Test Generator

Homework Assignments

_____

_____

_____

_____

_____

Other Teaching Materials

_____

_____

_____

_____

_____

Camouflaging the Chimera / Deciding

Core Objectives
- Understand and appreciate two poems about the Vietnam War
- Understand the speaker in poetry
- Examine structure in poetry

MISSOURI PLANNER
Grade-Level Expectations
R1.C, R1.D, R1.F, R1.G, R1.H, R1.I, R2.A, R2.C, W1.A, IL1.A, IL1.B, IL1.C

Integrating Skills
Grammar
- Punctuation: Capitalization

Vocabulary
- Using Context to Understand Figurative Language

Preparing to Read
____ Comparing Literature
____ Build Background
____ Focus Your Reading
  Literary Analysis: Speaker in Poetry ❑ Unit Seven Resource Book: Literary Analysis SkillBuilder, p. 22
  Active Reading: Structure in Poetry ❑ Unit Seven Resource Book: Active Reading SkillBuilder, p. 21

Teaching the Literature
____ Reading the Selection ❑ PE pp. 1111–1117

Thinking Through the Literature
____ Connect to the Literature
____ Think Critically ❑ Reading and Critical Thinking Transparencies, T15, T17
____ Extend Interpretations
____ Literary Analysis: Speaker in Poetry

Choices and Challenges
Writing Options
____ Points of Comparison

Inquiry and Research
____ Environmental Effects of War

Camouflaging the Chimera / Deciding

Teaching Options (from Teacher's Edition)

Mini Lessons

Vocabulary Strategy

____ Using Context to Understand Figurative Language   ❑ Vocabulary Transparencies and Copymasters, C93

Grammar

____ Punctuation: Capitalization   ❑ Grammar Transparencies and Copymasters, C145, C171

Informal Assessment

____ Letter Writing

Assessment

____ Selection Test   ❑ Formal Assessment: Selection Test, pp. 209–210

____ Test Generator

Homework Assignments

_____

_____

_____

_____

_____

Other Teaching Materials

_____

_____

_____

_____

_____

At the Justice Department, November 15, 1969

Core Objectives
- Understand and appreciate a protest poem
- Understand the elements of style
- Make inferences about meaning

> **MISSOURI PLANNER**
> Grade-Level Expectations
> R1.C, R1.D, R1.F, R1.G, R1.H, R1.I, R2.A, R2.C,
> W1.A, IL1.A, IL1.B, IL1.C

Integrating Skills
Grammar
- Varying Sentence Closers

Preparing to Read
____ Comparing Literature
____ Build Background
____ Focus Your Reading
    Literary Analysis: Style   ❑ Unit Seven Resource Book: Literary Analysis SkillBuilder, p. 24
    Active Reading: Making Inferences ❑ Unit Seven Resource Book: Active Reading SkillBuilder, p. 23
      About Meaning

Teaching the Literature
____ Reading the Selection   ❑ PE pp. 1118–1121

Thinking Through the Literature
____ Connect to the Literature
____ Think Critically   ❑ Reading and Critical Thinking Transparencies, T7, T52
____ Extend Interpretations
____ Literary Analysis: Style   ❑ Literary Analysis Transparencies, T23

Choices and Challenges
Writing Options
____ TV Script
____ Antiwar Storyboard
____ Points of Comparison

Activities and Explorations
____ Opinion Poster
____ War Debate

Inquiry and Research
____ Impact of Antiwar Protests

At the Justice Department,
November 15, 1969

Teaching Options (from Teacher's Edition)

Mini Lessons

Grammar

___ Varying Sentence Closers

❏ Grammar Transparencies and Copymasters, C172

Informal Assessment

___ Writing a Summary

Assessment

___ Selection Test

___ Part Test

___ Test Generator

❏ Formal Assessment: Selection Test, pp. 211–212

❏ Formal Assessment: Unit Seven, Part 1 Test, pp. 213–214

Homework Assignments	Other Teaching Materials
_____	_____
_____	_____
_____	_____
_____	_____
_____	_____

Multimedia Exhibit

Prompt

Create a multimedia exhibit about
a topic that interests you.

```
┌─────────────────────────────────────┐
│          MISSOURI PLANNER            │
│      Grade-Level Expectations        │
│  R3.D, W2.D, W2.E, W2.F              │
└─────────────────────────────────────┘
```

Preparing to Read

____ Introduction

____ Basics in a Box

____ Presenting the Guidelines and Standards

____ Analyzing a Multimedia Exhibit
"America at War"

Creating

____ **Planning the Multimedia Exhibit**   ❏ Unit Seven Resource Book: Planning Your Exhibit, p. 26

____ **Preparing the Exhibit**   ❏ Unit Seven Resource Book: Preparing Your Exhibit, p. 27

____ **Peer Review**   ❏ Unit Seven Resource Book: Peer Response Guide, pp. 28–29
Ask Your Peer Reader

____ **Refining the Exhibit**   ❏ Unit Seven Resource Book: Refining Your Exhibit, p. 30
                                                  ❏ Unit Seven Resource Book: Standards for Evaluation, p. 31

____ **Reflecting**

Homework Assignments

_____

_____

_____

_____

_____

Other Teaching Materials

_____

_____

_____

_____

_____

Letter from Birmingham Jail

Core Objectives
- Understand a historic letter
- Identify and examine allusion
- Understand logical argument: deduction and induction

```
┌─────────────────────────────────────┐
│          MISSOURI PLANNER             │
│       Grade-Level Expectations        │
│  R1.C, R1.D, R1.F, R1.G, R1.H, R1.I, R2.A, R2.C, │
│  R3.C, W1.A, W3.C, IL1.A, IL1.B, IL1.C │
└─────────────────────────────────────┘
```

Integrating Skills

Grammar	**Vocabulary**
▪ Verbs: Voice and Mood	▪ Using Context Clues ▪ Latin Roots

Preparing to Read
____ Connect to Your Life
____ Build Background
____ Vocabulary Preview: Using Context Clues   ❑ Unit Seven Resource Book: Words to Know SkillBuilder, p. 37
____ Focus Your Reading
     Literary Analysis: Allusion   ❑ Unit Seven Resource Book: Literary Analysis SkillBuilder, p. 36
     Active Reading: Logical Argument: Induction   ❑ Unit Seven Resource Book: Active Reading SkillBuilder, p. 35
     and Deduction

Teaching the Literature
                                            ❑ PE pp. 1136–1147
____ Reading the Selection   ❑ Unit Seven Resource Book: Summary, p. 34

Thinking Through the Literature
____ Connect to the Literature
____ Think Critically   ❑ Reading and Critical Thinking Transparencies, T21
____ Extend Interpretations
____ Literary Analysis: Allusion

Choices and Challenges
Writing Options
____ Defining a Hero
____ Editorial About King's Ideas
____ Compare-and-Contrast Essay

Activities and Explorations
____ Poster Design
____ Dramatic Skit
____ Multimedia Presentation

Inquiry and Research
____ Civil Rights Today

Vocabulary in Action
____ Meaning Clues
____ Synonyms

Letter from Birmingham Jail

Teaching Options (from Teacher's Edition)

Mini Lessons

Preteaching Vocabulary
____ Using Context Clues

Vocabulary Strategy
____ Latin Roots

❑ Vocabulary Transparencies and Copymasters, C94

Grammar
____ Verbs: Voice and Mood

❑ Grammar Transparencies and Copymasters, C119

Speaking and Listening
____ Persuasive Speech

Viewing and Representing
Art Appreciation
____ Photographs as Chronicles

Cross Curricular Link

History
____ Civil Rights Movement

Informal Assessment
____ Choosing the Best Summary

Assessment
____ Selection Quiz
____ Selection Test
____ Test Generator

❑ Formal Assessment: Selection Quiz, p. 38
❑ Formal Assessment: Selection Test, pp. 215–216

Homework Assignments

_____
_____
_____
_____
_____

Other Teaching Materials

_____
_____
_____
_____
_____

Wandering

Core Objectives
- Understand and appreciate a one-act drama
- Examine tone and dialogue
- Visualize stage directions

```
┌─────────────────────────────────────┐
│         MISSOURI PLANNER             │
│      Grade-Level Expectations        │
│ R1.C, R1.D, R1.E, R1.F, R1.G, R1.H, R1.I, R2.A, │
│ R2.C, W1.A, IL1.A, IL1.B, IL1.C      │
└─────────────────────────────────────┘
```

Integrating Skills

Grammar
- Prepositional Phrases

Vocabulary
- Using Context Clues

Preparing to Read
____ Connect to Your Life
____ Build Background
____ Vocabulary Preview: Using Context Clues   ❏ Unit Seven Resource Book: Words to Know SkillBuilder, p. 42
____ Focus Your Reading
      Literary Analysis: Tone and Dialogue   ❏ Unit Seven Resource Book: Literary Analysis SkillBuilder, p. 41
      Active Reading: Visualizing Stage Directions   ❏ Unit Seven Resource Book: Active Reading SkillBuilder, p. 40

Teaching the Literature   ❏ PE pp. 1150–1156
____ Reading the Selection   ❏ Unit Seven Resource Book: Summary, p. 39

Thinking Through the Literature
____ Connect to the Literature
____ Think Critically   ❏ Reading and Critical Thinking Transparencies, T8
____ Extend Interpretations
____ Literary Analysis: Tone and Dialogue   ❏ Literary Analysis Transparencies, T19

Choices and Challenges
Writing Options
____ Drama Review
____ Play Outline

Inquiry and Research
____ Youth Counterculture

Vocabulary in Action
____ Context Clues

Wandering

Teaching Options (from Teacher's Edition)

Mini Lessons

Preteaching Vocabulary
____ Using Context Clues

Grammar
____ Proliferating Prepositional Phrases   ❏ Grammar Transparencies and Copymasters, C173

Speaking and Listening
____ Drama Reenactment

Cross Curricular Link

History
____ A Time of Upheaval and Protest

Informal Assessment
____ Self-Assessment

Assessment

____ Selection Quiz   ❏ Unit Seven Resource Book: Selection Quiz, p. 43
____ Selection Test   ❏ Formal Assessment: Selection Test, pp. 217–218
____ Test Generator

Homework Assignments	**Other Teaching Materials**

The Writer in the Family

Core Objectives
- Understand and appreciate a short story
- Understand plot development
- Draw conclusions about character

Integrating Skills

Grammar
- Unnecessary Commas
- Active vs. Passive Voice

Vocabulary
- Using Context Clues

> **MISSOURI PLANNER**
> Grade-Level Expectations
> R1.C, R1.D, R1.E, R1.F, R1.G, R1.H, R1.I, R2.A, R2.C, W1.A

Preparing to Read
____ Connect to Your Life
____ Build Background
____ Vocabulary Preview: Using Context Clues   ❑ Unit Seven Resource Book: Words to Know SkillBuilder, p. 47
____ Focus Your Reading
    Literary Analysis: Plot Development   ❑ Unit Seven Resource Book: Literary Analysis SkillBuilder, p. 46
    Active Reading: Drawing Conclusions About   ❑ Unit Seven Resource Book: Active Reading SkillBuilder, p. 45
    Characters

Teaching the Literature
    ❑ PE pp. 1157–1167
____ Reading the Selection   ❑ Unit Seven Resource Book: Summary, p. 44

Thinking Through the Literature
____ Connect to the Literature
____ Think Critically   ❑ Reading and Critical Thinking Transparencies, T4, T54
____ Extend Interpretations
____ Literary Analysis: Plot Development

Choices and Challenges

Writing Options
____ True Obituary
____ Definition of Success

Activities and Explorations
____ Mourning Rituals

Inquiry and Research
____ Mourning Rituals

Vocabulary in Action
____ Context Clues

The Writer in the Family

Teaching Options (from Teacher's Edition)

Mini Lessons

Preteaching Vocabulary
____ Using Context Clues

Grammar
____ Unnecessary Commas   ❏ Grammar Transparencies and Copymasters, C155
____ Voice: Active vs. Passive   ❏ Grammar Transparencies and Copymasters, C68

Workplace Link
____ Writing a Business Letter

Informal Assessment
____ Retelling

Assessment
____ Selection Quiz   ❏ Unit Seven Resource Book: Selection Quiz, p. 48
____ Selection Test   ❏ Formal Assessment: Selection Test, pp. 219–220
____ Test Generator

Homework Assignments	Other Teaching Materials
_____	_____
_____	_____
_____	_____
_____	_____
_____	_____

Teenage Wasteland

Core Objectives
- Understand and appreciate a short story
- Understand protagonist and antagonist
- Recognize important details

> **MISSOURI PLANNER**
> Grade-Level Expectations
> R1.C, R1.D, R1.F, R1.G, R1.H, R1.I, R2.A, R2.C, W1.A

Integrating Skills

Grammar
- Verbs: Progressive and Emphatic Forms

Vocabulary
- Synonyms and Antonyms

Preparing to Read
____ Connect to Your Life
____ Build Background
____ Vocabulary Preview: Synonyms and
      Antonyms
____ Focus Your Reading
      Literary Analysis: Character: Protagonist
        and Antagonist
      Active Reading: Recognizing Important Details

❑ Unit Seven Resource Book: Words to Know SkillBuilder, p. 52

❑ Unit Seven Resource Book: Literary Analysis SkillBuilder, p. 51

❑ Unit Seven Resource Book: Active Reading SkillBuilder, p. 50

Teaching the Literature
____ Reading the Selection

❑ PE pp. 1168–1179
❑ Unit Seven Resource Book: Summary, p. 49

Thinking Through the Literature
____ Connect to the Literature
____ Think Critically
____ Extend Interpretations
____ Literary Analysis: Protagonist and Antagonist

❑ Reading and Critical Thinking Transparencies, T9

Choices and Challenges

Writing Options
____ Rewritten Episodes
____ Persuasive Speech

Activities and Explorations
____ Dramatic Scene

Vocabulary in Action
____ Synonyms and Antonyms

Teenage Wasteland

Teaching Options (from Teacher's Edition)

Mini Lessons

Preteaching Vocabulary
____ Synonyms and Antonyms

Grammar
____ Verbs: Progressive and Emphatic
Forms

❑ Grammar Transparencies and Copymasters, C118

Speaking and Listening
____ Role-Playing

Viewing and Representing
Art Appreciation
____ *Table with Fruit* by David Park
____ *Girl Looking at Landscape* by Richard Diebenkorn

Informal Assessment
____ Self-Assessment

Assessment
____ Selection Quiz
____ Selection Test
____ Test Generator

❑ Unit Seven Resource Book: Selection Quiz, p. 53
❑ Formal Assessment: Selection Test, pp. 221–222

Homework Assignments
_____
_____
_____
_____
_____

Other Teaching Materials
_____
_____
_____
_____
_____

Separating

Core Objectives
- Understand and appreciate a short story
- Understand dramatic irony
- Make predictions

MISSOURI PLANNER
Grade-Level Expectations
R1.C, R1.D, R1.F, R1.G, R1.H, R1.I, R2.A, R2.C, W1.A

Integrating Skills

Grammar
- Advanced Sentences: Sentence Openers
- Advanced Sentences: Periodic Sentences

Vocabulary
- Context Clues

Preparing to Read
____ Connect to Your Life
____ Build Background
____ Vocabulary Preview: Context Clues   ❑ Unit Seven Resource Book: Words to Know SkillBuilder, p. 57
____ Focus Your Reading
     Literary Analysis: Dramatic Irony   ❑ Unit Seven Resource Book: Literary Analysis SkillBuilder, p. 56
     Active Reading: Making Predictions   ❑ Unit Seven Resource Book: Active Reading SkillBuilder, p. 55

Teaching the Literature
        ❑ PE pp. 1180–1193
____ Reading the Selection   ❑ Unit Seven Resource Book: Summary, p. 54

Thinking Through the Literature
____ Connect to the Literature
____ Think Critically   ❑ Reading and Critical Thinking Transparencies, T2
____ Extend Interpretations
____ Literary Analysis: Dramatic Irony

Choices and Challenges

Writing Options
____ Diary Entry
____ Character Analysis
____ Story Forecast

Activities and Explorations
____ Staging a Scene

Vocabulary in Action
____ Synonyms
____ Assessment Practice

Separating

....

Teaching Options (from Teacher's Edition)

Mini Lessons

Preteaching Vocabulary
____ Using Context Clues

Speaking and Listening
____ Performing a Scene

Grammar
____ Advanced Sentences: Sentence Openers   ❑ Grammar Transparencies and Copymasters, C174

____ Advanced Sentences: Periodic Sentences   ❑ Grammar Transparencies and Copymasters, C175

Viewing and Representing
Art Appreciation
____ *Frank Wallace* and *Claire White* by Fairfield Porter

Cross Curricular Links

Social Studies
____ Divorce Law

Workplace
____ Preparing for Projects

Informal Assessment

____ Adapting Point of View
____ Making Predictions

Assessment

____ Selection Quiz   ❑ Unit Seven Resource Book: Selection Quiz, p. 58
____ Selection Test   ❑ Formal Assessment: Selection Test, pp. 223–224
____ Test Generator

Homework Assignments	Other Teaching Materials
_____	_____
_____	_____
_____	_____
_____	_____
_____	_____

Mexicans Begin Jogging / Legal Alien

Core Objectives
- Understand and appreciate two contemporary poems
- Examine tone in poetry
- Compare writers' attitudes

┌─────────────────────────────────────┐
│ **MISSOURI PLANNER** │
│ Grade-Level Expectations │
│ R1.C, R1.D, R1.F, R1.G, R1.H, R1.I, R2.A, R2.C, │
│ W1.A, IL1.A, IL1.B, IL1.C │
└─────────────────────────────────────┘

Integrating Skills

Grammar
- Varying Types of Sentences

Vocabulary
- Connotation

Preparing to Read
____ Connect to Your Life
____ Build Background
____ Focus Your Reading
      Literary Analysis: Tone   ❑ Unit Seven Resource Book: Literary Analysis SkillBuilder, p. 60
      Active Reading: Comparing Writers' Attitudes   ❑ Unit Seven Resource Book: Active Reading SkillBuilder, p. 59

Teaching the Literature
____ Reading the Selection   ❑ PE pp. 1194–1199

Thinking Through the Literature
____ Connect to the Literature
____ Think Critically   ❑ Reading and Critical Thinking Transparencies, T23
____ Extend Interpretations
____ Literary Analysis: Tone

Choices and Challenges

Writing Options
____ Guest Editorial

Inquiry and Research
____ The Title "Legal Alien"

Art Connection
____ Photographs

Mexicans Begin Jogging / Legal Alien

Teaching Options (from Teacher's Edition)

Mini Lessons

Vocabulary Strategy

____ Interpreting the Connotative Power of Words

❏ Vocabulary Transparencies and Copymasters, C95

Grammar

____ Varying Types of Sentences

❏ Grammar Transparencies and Copymasters, C176

Assessment

____ Selection Test

____ Test Generator

❏ Formal Assessment: Selection Test, pp. 225–226

<table>
<tr><td>

Homework Assignments

_____

_____

_____

_____

_____

</td><td>

Other Teaching Materials

_____

_____

_____

_____

_____

</td></tr>
</table>

Hostage

Core Objectives
- Understand and appreciate a short story
- Understand character
- Make judgments about character

MISSOURI PLANNER
Grade-Level Expectations
R1.C, R1.D, R1.E, R1.F, R1.G, R1.H, R1.I, R2.A, R2.C, W1.A, W3.C, IL1.A, IL1.B, IL1.C

Integrating Skills

Grammar
- Interrupting Elements

Vocabulary
- Using Context Clues
- Synonyms and Antonyms

Preparing to Read
____ Comparing Literature
____ Vocabulary Preview: Using Context Clues   ❑ Unit Seven Resource Book: Words to Know SkillBuilder, p. 64
____ Focus Your Reading
        Literary Analysis: Character   ❑ Unit Seven Resource Book: Literary Analysis SkillBuilder, p. 63
        Active Reading: Making Judgments   ❑ Unit Seven Resource Book: Active Reading SkillBuilder, p. 62
            About Character

Teaching the Literature   ❑ PE pp. 1200–1214
____ Reading the Selection   ❑ Unit Seven Resource Book: Summary, p. 61

Thinking Through the Literature
____ Connect to the Literature
____ Think Critically   ❑ Reading and Critical Thinking Transparencies, T5, T57, T36–38
____ Extend Interpretations
____ Literary Analysis: Character: Tragic Hero   ❑ Literary Analysis Transparencies, T6

Choices and Challenges

Writing Options
____ Character Sketch
____ Expository Essay
____ Literary Review
____ Points of Comparison

Activities and Explorations
____ Role-Play
____ Drawing
____ Debate

Inquiry and Research
____ Crime Statistics

Vocabulary in Action
____ Synonyms and Antonyms
____ Context Clues

____ **Author Activity**

Selection Lesson Plan (continued)

Hostage

Teaching Options (from Teacher's Edition)

Mini Lessons

Preteaching Vocabulary
____ Using Context Clues

Vocabulary Strategy
____ Synonyms and Antonyms   ❑ Vocabulary Transparencies and Copymasters, C96

Grammar
____ Interrupting Elements: Descriptions   ❑ Grammar Transparencies and Copymasters, C177
That Split Subject and Verb

Speaking and Listening
____ Storytelling
____ Interviewing

Viewing and Representing
Art Appreciation

Informal Assessment
____ Understanding Character
____ Choosing the Best Theme

Assessment
____ Selection Quiz   ❑ Unit Seven Resource Book: Selection Quiz, p. 65
____ Selection Test   ❑ Formal Assessment: Selection Test, pp. 227–228
____ Part Test
____ Test Generator

Homework Assignments

Other Teaching Materials

Mother Tongue

Core Objectives
- Understand and appreciate a personal essay
- Identify main ideas and supporting details

Integrating Skills

Grammar	Vocabulary
■ Cohesion	■ Using Context Clues

> **MISSOURI PLANNER**
> Grade-Level Expectations
> R1.C, R1.D, R1.E, R1.F, R1.G, R1.H, R1.I, R2.A, R2.C, W1.A, W3.C

Preparing to Read
____ Comparing Literature
____ Build Background
____ Vocabulary Preview: Using Context Clues   ❏ Unit Seven Resource Book: Words to Know SkillBuilder, p. 69
____ Focus Your Reading
      Literary Analysis: Personal Essay   ❏ Unit Seven Resource Book: Literary Analysis SkillBuilder, p. 68
      Active Reading: Identifying Main Ideas and   ❏ Unit Seven Resource Book: Active Reading SkillBuilder, p. 67
        Supporting Details

Teaching the Literature
      ❏ PE pp. 1215–1222
____ Reading the Selection   ❏ Unit Seven Resource Book: Summary, p. 66

Thinking Through the Literature
____ Connect to the Literature
____ Think Critically   ❏ Reading and Critical Thinking Transparencies, T47, T55
____ Extend Interpretations
____ Literary Analysis: Personal Essay

Choices and Challenges
Writing Options
____ Story Evaluation
____ Points of Comparison

Vocabulary in Action
____ Context Clues

Author Activity
____ Tan's Short Stories

Teaching Options (from Teacher's Edition)

Mini Lessons

Preteaching Vocabulary
____ Using Context Clues

Grammar
____ Cohesion: Reader Expectation ❑ Grammar Transparencies and Copymasters, C178

Speaking and Listening
____ Effective Listening Skills: Role-Play

Informal Assessment
____ Letter of Complaint

Assessment
____ Selection Quiz ❑ Unit Seven Resource Book: Selection Quiz, p. 70
____ Selection Test ❑ Formal Assessment: Selection Test, pp. 229–230
____ Test Generator

Homework Assignments

_____

_____

_____

_____

_____

Other Teaching Materials

_____

_____

_____

_____

_____

The Latin Deli: An Ars Poetica

Core Objectives
- Understand and appreciate a poem about bicultural experience
- Understand and appreciate imagery
- Analyze descriptive details

MISSOURI PLANNER

Grade-Level Expectations

R1.C, R1.D, R1.F, R1.G, R1.H, R1.I, R2.A, R2.C, W1.A, IL1.A, IL1.B, IL1.C

Integrating Skills
Grammar
- Types of Pronouns

Preparing to Read
____ Comparing Literature
____ Build Background
____ Focus Your Reading
     Literary Analysis: Imagery   ❑ Unit Seven Resource Book: Literary Analysis SkillBuilder, p. 72
     Active Reading: Analyzing Descriptive Details   ❑ Unit Seven Resource Book: Active Reading SkillBuilder, p. 71

Teaching the Literature
____ Reading the Selection   ❑ PE pp. 1223–1226

Thinking Through the Literature
____ Connect to the Literature
____ Think Critically   ❑ Reading and Critical Thinking Transparencies, T48, T46, T51
____ Extend Interpretations
____ Literary Analysis: Imagery

Choices and Challenges
Writing Options
____ Description of a Place
____ Grocery List
____ Points of Comparison

Activities and Explorations
____ Dramatic Skit
____ Advertising Flyer

Inquiry and Research
____ Latin American Cookbook

Author Activity
____ Poetry Slam

Selection Lesson Plan (continued)

The Latin Deli: An Ars Poetica

Teaching Options (from Teacher's Edition)

Mini Lesson

Grammar

___ Types of Pronouns   ❑ Grammar Transparencies and Copymasters, T39, T40, C65

Assessment

___ Selection Test   ❑ Formal Assessment: Selection Test, pp. 231–232
___ Test Generator

Homework Assignments	**Other Teaching Materials**
_____	_____
_____	_____
_____	_____
_____	_____
_____	_____

Straw into Gold: The Metamorphosis
of the Everyday

Core Objectives
- Understand and appreciate a personal essay by a Latina writer
- Understand and appreciate voice
- Analyze structure

> **MISSOURI PLANNER**
> Grade-Level Expectations
> R1.C, R1.D, R1.F, R1.G, R1.H, R1.I, R2.A, R2.C, W1.A

Integrating Skills
Grammar
- Noun Phrases
- Style: Deliberate Fragments

Vocabulary
- Using Context Clues

Preparing to Read
____ Comparing Literature
____ Build Background
____ Vocabulary Preview: Using Context Clues   ❑ Unit Seven Resource Book: Words to Know SkillBuilder, p. 76
____ Focus Your Reading
    Literary Analysis: Voice   ❑ Unit Seven Resource Book: Literary Analysis SkillBuilder, p. 75
    Active Reading: Analyzing Structure   ❑ Unit Seven Resource Book: Active Reading SkillBuilder, p. 74

Teaching the Literature
    ❑ PE pp. 1227–1233
____ Reading the Selection   ❑ Unit Seven Resource Book: Summary, p. 73

Thinking Through the Literature
____ Connect to the Literature
____ Think Critically   ❑ Reading and Critical Thinking Transparencies, T15
____ Extend Interpretations
____ Literary Analysis: Voice   ❑ Literary Analysis Transparencies, T23

Choices and Challenges
Writing Options
____ Letter of Advice
____ Points of Comparison

Art Connection
____ *Olga* by Rufino Tomayo

Vocabulary in Action
____ Meaning Clues

Straw into Gold: The Metamorphosis of the Everyday

Teaching Options (from Teacher's Edition)

Mini Lessons

Preteaching Vocabulary
____ Using Context Clues

Grammar
____ Noun Phrases   ❏ Grammar Transparencies and Copymasters, C179
____ Style: Deliberate Fragments   ❏ Grammar Transparencies and Copymasters, C180

Viewing and Representing
Art Appreciation
____ *Olga* by Rufino Tamayo

Assessment

____ Selection Quiz   ❏ Formal Assessment: Selection Quiz, p. 77
____ Selection Test   ❏ Formal Assessment: Selection Test, pp 233–234
____ Part Test   ❏ Formal Assessment: Unit Seven, Part 2 Test, pp. 235–236
____ Test Generator

Homework Assignments

_____
_____
_____
_____
_____

Other Teaching Materials

_____
_____
_____
_____
_____

Selection Lesson Plan   *Name* _____ *Date* _____

....

Core Objectives

Integrating Skills
Grammar   Vocabulary

Preparing to Read
___ Connect to Your Life
___ Build Background
___ Preteaching Vocabulary
___ Focus Your Reading
    Literary Analysis:
    Active Reading:

Teaching the Literature
___ Reading the Selection

Thinking Through the Literature
___ Connect to the Literature
___ Think Critically
___ Extend Interpretations
___ Literary Analysis:

Choices and Challenges
___ Writing Options

___ Activities and Explorations

___ Inquiry and Research

___ Vocabulary in Action

___ Grammar in Context

___ Author Activity

___ Art Connection

Teaching Options (from Teacher's Edition)

Mini Lessons

Vocabulary Strategy

Speaking and Listening

Viewing and Representing: Art Appreciation

Grammar

Cross Curricular Links

Informal Assessment

Assessment

____ Selection Quiz

____ Selection Test

____ Part Test

____ Test Generator

Homework Assignments	Other Teaching Materials
_____	_____
_____	_____
_____	_____
_____	_____
_____	_____

Writing Prompt

Preparing to Read
____ Introduction
____ Basics in a Box
____ Using the Graphic
____ Presenting the Rubric

____ Analyzing a Student Model

Writing
____ Prewriting

____ Drafting

____ Peer Review

____ Revising

____ Editing and Proofreading

____ Reflecting

Homework Assignments
_____
_____
_____
_____
_____

Other Teaching Materials
_____
_____
_____
_____
_____

Missouri Content Standards, Grade 9–12

Reading

1. **Develop and apply skills and strategies to the reading process**

   A. Print Concepts

   B. Phonemic Awareness

   C. Phonics

   Apply decoding strategies to "problem-solve" unknown words when reading

   D. Fluency

   Read grade-level instructional text
   • with fluency, accuracy and appropriate expression
   • adjusting reading rate to difficulty and type of text

   E. Vocabulary

   Develop vocabulary through text, using
   • roots and affixes
   • context clues
   • glossary, dictionary and thesaurus

   F. Pre-Reading

   Apply pre-reading strategies to aid comprehension
   • access prior knowledge
   • preview
   • predict
   • set a purpose and rate for reading

   G. During Reading

   During reading, utilize strategies to
   • self-question and correct
   • infer
   • visualize
   • predict and check using cueing systems
      ♦ meaning
      ♦ structure
      ♦ visual

   H. Post-Reading

   Apply post-reading skills to comprehend and interpret text
   • question to clarify
   • reflect
   • analyze
   • draw conclusions
   • summarize
   • paraphrase

I. Making Connections

Compare, contrast, analyze and evaluate connections between
• information and relationships in various fiction and non-fiction works
• text ideas and own experiences
• text ideas and the world by analyzing and evaluating the relationship between literature and its historical period and culture

2. **Develop and apply skills and strategies to comprehend, analyze and evaluate fiction, poetry and drama from a variety of cultures and times**

A. Text Features

Locate
• interpret and apply information in title, table of contents and glossary
• and recognize the text features of fiction, poetry and drama in grade-level text

B. Literary Devices

Analyze and evaluate author's use of figurative language (emphasize **irony**), imagery and **sound devices** in poetry and prose

C. Text Elements

Use details from text to
• analyze character, plot, setting, point of view and development of theme
• evaluate proposed solutions
• analyze the development of a theme across genres
• evaluate the effect of **author's style** and complex literary techniques (including **tone**)

3. **Develop and apply skills and strategies to comprehend, analyze and evaluate nonfiction (such as biographies, newspapers, technical manuals) from a variety of cultures and times**

A. Text Features

Evaluate the author's use of text features to clarify meaning in multiple primary and/or secondary sources

B. Literary Devices

Analyze and evaluate author's use of figurative language (emphasize irony), imagery and sound devices in nonfiction text

C. Text Elements

Use details from text to
• analyze and evaluate the logic, reasonableness, and audience appeal of arguments in texts
• identify and analyze faulty reasoning and unfounded inferences
• evaluate for accuracy and adequacy of evidence
• analyze and evaluate the author's use of information and logic to express his or her ideas through
    ♦ word choice
    ♦ comprehensiveness of detail selection
    ♦ organizational patterns
• evaluate proposed solutions

D. Understanding Directions

Read and apply multistep directions to perform complex procedures and/or tasks

Writing

1. **Apply a writing process in composing text**

   A. Writing Process

      Follow a writing process to
      • independently create appropriate graphic organizers as needed
      • apply writing process to write effectively in various forms and types of writing

2. **Compose well-developed text using standard English conventions**

   A. Handwriting

   B. Capitalization

      Use conventions of capitalization in written text

   C. Punctuation

      In composing text, use
      • correct formatting (e.g., quotation marks, italics and underlining) in **citations**
      • hyphens for compound adjectives

   D. Parts of Speech

      Use parts of speech correctly in written text

   E. Spelling

      In writing, use dictionary, spell-check and other resources to spell correctly

   F. Sentence construction

      In composing text, use
      • a variety of sentence structure and length for stylistic effect
      • cohesive devices
      • **active voice** construction

3. **Write effectively in various forms and types of writing**

   A. Narrative and Descriptive Writing

      Write a personal narrative for real-life experiences (e.g., scholarships, applications and postsecondary/college essays)

   B. Note-Taking

      Routinely use an appropriate method for note-taking

   C. Expository and Persuasive Writing

      Write
      • multi-paragraph informative and persuasive essays with
        ♦ an effective thesis statement
        ♦ effective paragraphing
        ♦ convincing elaboration through specific and relevant details
        ♦ originality (freshness of thought) and individual perspective
        ♦ individual style and voice
        ♦ complex ideas in a sustained and compelling manner

- multi-paragraph texts that
    - ♦ interpret, evaluate or persuade
    - ♦ use specific **rhetorical devices**
    - ♦ use relevant evidence to defend a position
- a **reflective paper** that compares specific incidents and themes
- an analysis and/or evaluation on the use of imagery, language, themes, **stylistic devices** and tone in literature

D. Summary Writing

Write
- a multi-paragraph text that summarizes large amounts of information clearly and concisely
- complete research papers/projects that develop a thesis, contain information from multiple sources and conform to a **style manual** (e.g., APA, MLA)

E. Audience and Purpose

Compose texts
- for a variety of career and workplace communications (e.g., job application, **résumé,** cover letter, college application essay, thank-you note, follow-up note, forms, project proposal, brochure and/or concise directions)
- for various audiences and purposes, selecting and applying appropriate format, style, tone and point of view

Listening and Speaking

1. **Develop and apply effective listening skills and strategies**

    A. Purpose for Listening

    Listen
    - for enjoyment
    - for information
    - for directions
    - critically to summarize and evaluate communications that inform, persuade and entertain
    - to evaluate own and others' effectiveness in presentations and group discussions, using provided criteria
    - to evaluate the **validity** and **reliability** of speaker's message

    B. Listening Behavior

    Use active-listening behaviors (e.g., asks questions of speaker and uses body language and facial expressions to indicate agreement, disagreement or confusion)

2. **Develop and apply effective speaking skills and strategies for various audiences and purposes**

    A. Discussion and Presentation

    In discussions and presentations,
    - create concise presentations on a variety of topics
    - incorporate appropriate media or technology
    - respond to feedback
    - defend ideas
    - demonstrate **poise** and self-control

    B. Giving Directions

    Give clear and concise multi-step oral directions to perform complex procedures and/or tasks

Information Literacy

1. **Develop and apply effective research processes to gather, analyze and evaluate information**

   A. Research plan

      Develop an appropriate research plan to guide investigation and research of focus questions

   B. Acquire Information

      Locate and use multiple primary and secondary sources to
      • select relevant and credible information
      • evaluate reliability of information
      • evaluate reliability of sources

   C. Record Information

      Record relevant information from multiple primary and secondary sources

   D. Sources Consulted

      Cite sources of information using a standard method of documentation

2. **Develop and apply effective skills and strategies to analyze and evaluate oral and visual media**

   A. Media messages

      Analyze, describe and evaluate the elements of messages projected in various media (e.g., videos, pictures, websites, artwork, plays and/or news programs)